Finding Sherlock's London

Finding Sherlock's London
Travel Guide to over 200 Sites in London

Thomas Bruce Wheeler

iUNIVERSE, INC.
New York Lincoln Shanghai

Finding Sherlock's London
Travel Guide to over 200 Sites in London

iUniverse, Inc.

For information address:
iUniverse, Inc.
2021 Pine Lake Road, Suite 100
Lincoln, NE 68512
www.iuniverse.com

ISBN: 0-595-28114-1

Printed in the United States of America

Contents

INTRODUCTION~xi

London Underground Stations

- ALDGATE~3
- ALDGATE EAST~4
- ANGEL~4
- BAKER STREET~4
- BANK~6
- BARBICAN~7
- BLACKFRIARS~7
- BOND STREET~7
- BOROUGH~9
- BRIXTON~10
- CANNON STREET~11
- CHANCERY LANE~11
- CHARING CROSS~12
- CAMDEN TOWN~16
- CLAPHAM COMMON~16
- CLAPHAM NORTH~17
- CLAPHAM SOUTH~17
- COVENT GARDEN~17
- EDGWARE ROAD~18
- EMBANKMENT~19
- EUSTON~20
- EUSTON SQUARE~21

- FARRINGDON~21
- FULHAM BROADWAY~21
- GLOUCESTER ROAD~21
- GOODGE STREET~22
- GREEN PARK~22
- GREENWICH~24
- HAMMERSMITH~24
- HAMPSTEAD~25
- HARROW & WEALDSTONE~25
- HIGH STREET KENSINGTON~26
- HOLBORN~26
- ISLAND GARDENS (DOCKLANDS LIGHT RAILROAD)~27
- KENNINGTON~27
- KILBURN~27
- KING'S CROSS/ST. PANCRAS~28
- LANCASTER GATE~28
- LIMEHOUSE~28
- LIVERPOOL STREET~29
- MANSION HOUSE~29
- MARBLE ARCH~29
- MONUMENT~30
- MOORGATE~30
- NOTTING HILL GATE~30
- OLYMPIA~31
- OVAL~31
- OXFORD CIRCUS~32
- PADDINGTON~33
- PICCADILLY CIRCUS~34
- PIMLICO~36
- PUTNEY BRIDGE~36
- REGENT'S PARK~36

- RICHMOND~37
- ROTHERHITHE~37
- RUSSELL SQUARE~37
- SHADWELL~37
- SOUTH KENSINGTON~38
- ST JAMES'S PARK~38
- ST JOHN'S WOOD~38
- ST PAUL'S~38
- TEMPLE~39
- TOOTING BEC~40
- TOTTENHAM COURT ROAD~40
- TOWER HILL~40
- VAUXHALL~41
- VICTORIA~42
- WATERLOO~43
- WEST INDIA QUAY~43
- WESTMINSTER~44
- BRITRAIL STATIONS~46

Sherlock Holmes Adventures

- ABBEY GRANGE~51
- BERYL CORONET~51
- BLACK PETER~52
- BLANCHED SOLDIER~52
- BLUE CARBUNCLE~52
- BOSCOMBE VALLEY MYSTERY~54
- BRUCE-PARTINGTON PLANS~54
- CARDBOARD BOX~56
- CASE OF IDENTITY~57
- CHARLES AUGUSTUS MILVERTON~57
- CREEPING MAN~58

- DANCING MEN~58
- DEVIL'S FOOT~59
- DYING DETECTIVE~59
- EMPTY HOUSE~59
- ENGINEER'S THUMB~61
- FINAL PROBLEM~61
- FIVE ORANGE PIPS~63
- GOLDEN PINCE-NEZ~63
- GREEK INTERPRETER~63
- HIS LAST BOW~65
- HOUND OF THE BASKERVILLES~66
- ILLUSTRIOUS CLIENT~69
- LADY FRANCES CARFAX~71
- MAN WITH THE TWISTED LIP~72
- MAZARIN STONE~73
- MISSING THREE-QUARTER~74
- MUSGRAVE RITUAL~74
- NAVAL TREATY~75
- NOBLE BACHELOR~76
- NORWOOD BUILDER~77
- PRIORY SCHOOL~77
- PROBLEM OF THOR BRIDGE--78
- RED CIRCLE~78
- RED-HEADED LEAGUE~79
- RESIDENT PATIENT~80
- RETIRED COLOURMAN~80
- SCANDAL IN BOHEMIA~81
- SECOND STAIN~82
- SHOSCOMBE OLD PLACE~83
- SIGN OF FOUR~83
- SILVER BLAZE~87

- SIX NAPOLEONS~87
- SOLITARY CYCLIST~88
- SPECKLED BAND~89
- STOCK-BROKER'S CLERK~89
- STUDY IN SCARLET~90
- SUSSEX VAMPIRE~92
- THE "GLORIA SCOTT"~93
- THREE GABLES~93
- THREE GARRIDEBS~94
- VALLEY OF FEAR~94
- VEILED LODGER~95
- WISTERIA LODGE~95
- YELLOW FACE~96

INTRODUCTION

In his Sherlock Holmes adventures, Sir Arthur Conan Doyle has probably done more than any other writer, to form our image of Victorian London. In our mind's eye, we still see the sinister, fog-bound city that was the center of the Empire. Although not entirely true, readers have come to think of the Sherlock Holmes' adventures, as London stories.

Holmes and Watson traveled all over Greater London. Today, time, the Blitz, and urban redevelopment have taken their toll, but much of what Sherlock "saw" is still there. Conan Doyle was unusually precise in his London addresses and locations, only occasionally disguising a site. However, many times, he gave enough clues to help us find these "hidden" locations.

The task of writing this book was further complicated by street name changes and renumbering. However, with humble detective skills, a 1902 London street map, and a large magnifying glass, I was able to identify over 200 Sherlockian sites in modern London. To help you visit these places, I have cross-referenced them by adventure, and by the closest modern underground station. The sites are mentioned in fifty-five of the Sherlock Holmes stories, and to see them all, you would have to visit seventy underground stations and twelve metropolitan BritRail stations.

Essentially, *Finding Sherlock's London* is a London gazetteer for Sherlock Holmes enthusiasts. To get the most out of it, re-read your favorite Sherlock Holmes adventures before you leave home, and bring along a pocket magnifying glass. After you arrive in London, buy a modern street guide (for which you will need the magnifying glass), and a TravelCard for unlimited travel on London's Underground and red buses. Then, enjoy—the game is afoot!

©2004—Thomas Bruce Wheeler

London Underground Stations

ALDGATE UNDERGROUND STATION

ALDGATE UNDERGROUND STATION—EC3 In *The Bruce-Partington Plans*, the body of Arthur Cadogan West was found near the tracks, just outside Aldgate Station. They thought he had been thrown from the train, but there was no ticket in his pockets.

FENCHURCH STREET—EC3 In *A Case of Identity*, Mary Sutherland's stepfather, James Windibank, worked for Westhouse and Marbank, the great claret importers of Fenchurch Street.

HOUNDSDITCH—EC3 In *A Study in Scarlet*, Mrs. Sawyer said she lived near Houndsditch. Holmes tried to follow her. When he reached the address, he found that it belonged to a respectable paperhanger named Keswick, who had never heard of Mrs. Sawyer.

LEADENHALL STREET—EC3 In *A Case of Identity*, Hosmer Angel, who in reality was Mary Sutherland's stepfather in disguise, was supposedly a cashier in an office in Leadenhall Street. Mary didn't know which office.

LLOYD'S OF LONDON—Fenchurch Street EC3 In *The Five Orange Pips*, Holmes spent the day at Lloyd's, going over their files to trace the ship, "Lone Star."

MINCING LANE—EC3 In *The Sussex Vampire*, Robert Ferguson, of Ferguson and Muirhead, tea brokers of Mincing Lane, was referred to Holmes on a matter of vampires. Holmes looked under V in his great index volume.

ALDGATE EAST UNDERGROUND STATION

COMMERCIAL STREET (ROAD)—E1 In *The Creeping Man,* Holmes stopped at a post office to send off a telegram. Mercer's reply reached him that evening. It read: "HAVE VISITED THE COMMERCIAL ROAD AND SEEN DORAK. SUAVE PERSON, BOHEMIAN, ELDERLY. KEEPS LARGE GENERAL STORE."

ANGEL UNDERGROUND STATION

PENTONVILLE—N1 This is the site of the Pentonville Prison, which was built in 1842. In *The Blue Carbuncle,* James Ryder's friend Maudsley had served time in Pentonville.

BAKER STREET UNDERGROUND STATION

31 (221B) BAKER STREET—W1 In *A Study in Scarlet,* Holmes and Watson's lodging on Baker Street was described as "a couple of comfortable bedrooms and a single large airy sitting-room, cheerfully furnished, and illuminated by two broad windows." In *The Five Orange Pips,* Watson mentions, "Holmes was already at breakfast when I came down." This indicates that Watson's bedroom was on the floor above. In *The Mazarin Stone,* we further learn that Holmes's bedroom had three doors: one leading to the sitting-room, a second exited into the hallway, where Holmes could see arriving guests, and a hidden third door that opened behind the curtains in the sitting-room.

Today, Baker Street has been extended, and the numbering changed from Sherlock's time. In *The Empty House,* we learn that Camden House was across the street from the old 221B. Since the Camden House location can be calculated rather precisely, the most likely location of 221B was the house formerly at today's #31 Baker Street.

32 or 34 BAKER STREET (CAMDEN HOUSE)—W1 In *The Empty House,* Holmes and Watson passed from Manchester Street to Blandford Street, en-route to Camden House.

Based on the route described, and other clues, the most likely location of Camden House was either today's #32 or #34 Baker Street.

BAKER STREET (METROPOLITAN) UNDERGROUND STATION—W1 In T*he Beryl Coronet,* Watson noticed a gentleman coming towards 221b Baker Street from the direction of the "Metropolitan Station." It was Alexander Holder, of the banking firm of Holder & Stevenson. The Baker Street Underground Station is on the Metropolitan Line, and Watson referred to it as the "Metropolitan" Station.

At the Marylebone exit of the Baker Street Station, there is a statue of Sherlock Holmes. Executed by John Doubleday, the work was commissioned by the Sherlock Holmes Society of London, and erected in 1999.

ABBEY NATIONAL BUILDING SOCIETY—Abbey House, 221 Baker Street, W1 On the west side of Baker Street, across and up from the Baker Street exit of the Underground Station, is Abbey House, the home of the Abbey National Building Society. The building, which stretches from 215 to 235, encompasses a famous address—221 Baker Street. Letters addressed to 221B Baker Street are delivered to Abbey House. The volume of mail is so great, that the Building Society had to assign a person to act as "Sherlock Holmes's secretary." Of course, these are all "modern" addresses, and do not reflect the location of the 221B Baker Street described in the Sherlock Holmes' adventures.

The nearby Sherlock Holmes Museum, which received permission from the Westminster Council to call its address 221B, is really located at 239 Baker Street.

BLANDFORD STREET—W1 In *The Empty House,* Holmes and Watson turned left from Manchester Street to Blandford Street on their way to Camden House.

SHERLOCK HOLMES HOTEL—108 Baker Street, W1 If you need a break from your exploration of Sherlock's London, you may want to stop at the Sherlock Holmes Hotel. In Dr. Watson's Pub, they welcome non-residents for drinks and pub grub, while more formal meals are available in Moriarty's Restaurant.

SHERLOCK HOLMES MEMORABILIA COMPANY—230 Baker Street, NW1 This shop offers a good selection of Holmes memorabilia, including items from the BBC series starring Jeremy Brent. They are expanding to new locations, so call ahead.

SHERLOCK HOLMES MUSEUM—239 (221B) Baker Street, NW1 This period townhouse is a good place to start your search for Sherlock's London. The ground floor has a memorabilia gift shop, and the upper floors are furnished as Conan Doyle described Holmes and Watson's digs.

SHERLOCK HOLMES WALKING TOUR—London Walks, Tel: 7624-3978 "Shall they not always live in Baker Street?" Join this walking tour of the Sherlock Holmes sites near 221B Baker Street. Every Tuesday, the group assembles at the Baker Street exit of the Baker Street Underground Station at 1:30PM. Call in advance to see if the times have changed.

MANCHESTER STREET—W1 In *The Empty House,* Holmes and Watson drove on Manchester Street on their way to Camden House. There they lay in wait for Colonel Sebastian Moran.

BANK UNDERGROUND STATION

LOMBARD STREET—EC3 After being let go from his billet at Coxon & Woodhouse's, Hall Pycroft, *The Stock-Broker's Clerk,* found a position at the great stock-brokerage firm of Mawson & Williams in Lombard Street.

OLD JEWRY—EC2 The firm of Morrison, Morrison and Dodd was located at No. 46 Old Jewry. In *The Sussex Vampire,* they remembered Holmes's successful action in the case of "The Matilda Briggs", and referred Mr. Ferguson.

THREADNEEDLE STREET—EC2 In *The Beryl Coronet,* Holder and Stevenson, the second largest private banking firm in the City, was located in Threadneedle Street.

In *The Man with the Twisted Lip,* Boone spent his days in Threadneedle Street, selling wax vestas.

THROGMORTON STREET—EC2 In *The Blanched Soldier,* James M. Dodd was a stock-broker in Throgmorton Street.

BARBICAN UNDERGROUND STATION

BARBICAN (ALDERSGATE) UNDERGROUND STATION—EC3 In *The Red-headed League,* Holmes and Watson got off the underground at the Aldersgate Station (now called the Barbican Station). From there they made their way to Jabez Wilson's small pawnshop. Holmes thumped the pavement with his stick, testing for tunnels.

BLACKFRIARS UNDERGROUND STATION

POPPINS (POPE'S) COURT—EC4 Poppins Court, at the eastern end of Fleet Street, was called Pope's Court in *The Red-headed League.* Duncan Ross, alias: William Morris, advertised for all red-headed men to apply at the offices of the League, No. 7 Pope's Court, just off Fleet Street.

BOND STREET UNDERGROUND STATION

BOND STREET—W1 John Straker, alias William Derbyshire, purchased an expensive costume from Madame Lesurier, a milliner in Bond Street. The receipt gave Holmes a clue that helped solve the *Silver Blaze* mystery.

In *The Hound of the Baskervilles,* while waiting for young Cartwright's report, Holmes and Watson spent the afternoon in the Bond Street picture galleries. Holmes was absorbed in the works of the modern Belgian masters.

BROOK STREET—W1 Blessington, *The Resident Patient,* set up Dr. Percy Trevelyan in a house at No. 403 Brook Street. Later Blessington was murdered, and Holmes revealed that he was really Sutton, the bank robber and informant.

CLARIDGE'S (HOTEL), Brook Street—W1 In *His Last Bow,* after capturing Von Bork, Holmes offered to shave off his goatee before reappearing as himself at Claridge's.

In *The Problem of Thor Bridge,* J. Neil Gibson wrote Holmes from Claridge's.

GROSVENOR SQUARE—W1 In *The Three Gables,* Holmes and Watson went to see Isadora Klein, the celebrated Spanish beauty. She was the widow of the sugar king, and lived in one of the finest corner-houses on Grosvenor Square.

MARYLEBONE LANE—W1 In *The Final Problem,* Holmes passed the corner which leads from Bentinck to the Welbeck Street crossing. He was almost hit by a two-horse van that dashed round by Marylebone Lane, and was gone in an instant.

OXFORD STREET—W1 In the 1890's, Oxford Street was as busy as it is today. We know that Holmes did his banking there, because in *The Adventure of the Priory School,* Holmes deposited the Duke's check in his Oxford Street branch bank.

In *The Disappearance of Lady Frances Carfax,* Watson bought his boots at Latimer's in Oxford Street.

In *The Hound of the Baskervilles,* it was mentioned that both Holmes and Watson used Bradley's in Oxford Street as their tobacconist. They supplied Holmes with his shag, and Watson with his cigarettes. Later, Dr. Mortimer and Baskerville walked down Oxford Street to Regent Street on their way to Northumberland. Holmes and Watson trailed behind, to see who was following Baskerville.

In *The Greek Interpreter,* Mr. Melas was picked up at his Pall Mall lodgings. The four-wheeler carriage started off through Charing Cross, up Shaftesbury Avenue to Oxford Street. When he commented that this was a roundabout way to Kensington, the windows were covered.

QUEEN ANNE STREET—W1 In the case of *The Illustrious Client,* Watson, who Sherlock called his "Boswell", had his surgery at No. 9 Queen Anne Street. Conan Doyle located the surgery there as a tribute to James Boswell, who lived in Queen Anne Street, when he wrote his *Life of Samuel Johnson.*

SOTHEBY'S AUCTION HOUSE, New Bond Street—W1 In *The Illustrious Client,* Watson, posing as Dr. Hill Barton, took the blue Ming saucer to Baron Gruner's. If pressed on a price, Watson was to suggest that Sotheby's or Christie's set the value.

VERE STREET—W1 In *The Final Problem,* a brick fell from a Vere Street building, shattering at Holmes's feet. This was just after the near "accident" at Bentinck and Welbeck streets. Now Holmes was sure that Professor Moriarty was behind the incidents.

WELBECK and BENTINCK STREETS—W1 In *The Final Problem,* Holmes was nearly killed by a two-horse van, at the intersection of Welbeck and Bentinck Streets. Holmes thought that Professor Moriarty's hand was behind it.

BOROUGH UNDERGROUND STATION

SOUTHWARK—SE1 In *The Hound of the Baskervilles,* Holmes located the driver of the cab that had been following Dr. Mortimer and Sir Henry. The drivers name was John Clayton, who lived in the Borough of Southwark. Holmes made a note of it.

BRIXTON UNDERGROUND STATION

BRIXTON ROAD—SW9 In *The Six Napoleons,* Dr. Barnicot, an admirer of Napoleon, bought two plaster busts from Morse Hudson. The busts were both smashed, one in Barnicot's Lower Brixton Road office.

In *The Greek Interpreter,* J. Davenport, of Lower Brixton Road, answered Mycroft Holmes's advertisement in the Daily News.

In *A Study in Scarlet,* Holmes and Watson passed Brixton Road on their way to No. 3 Lauriston Gardens. Tobias Gregson, "the smartest of the Scotland Yarders," had asked them to examine the site of Enoch J. Drebber's murder.

In *The Disappearance Of Lady Frances Carfax,* Holmes and Watson used a route along Brixton Road to visit Dr. Shlessinger house in Poultney Square.

In *The Blue Carbuncle,* Mrs. Oakshott lived at No. 117 Brixton Road. She sold her "city" geese to Mr. Breckinridge of Covent Garden, not knowing that her brother had stuffed the jewel into the gullet of one of them.

CAMBERWELL—SE5 In *A Study in Scarlet,* John Underwood, a haberdasher on Camberwell Road, sold a hat to Enoch J. Drebber. Drebber, who was later found dead at No. 3 Lauriston Gardens.

In *The Valley of Fear,* Holmes corresponded with Fred Porlock through the Camberwell post office. Porlock was an associate of Professor Moriarty. Today, the Camberwell post office is in Orpheus Street, SE5.

In *The Sign of Four,* Miss Morstan lived with Mrs. Cecil Forrester in Lower Camberwell. With a twinkle in his eyes, Holmes noted that Watson was eager to visit her there.

In *A Case of Identity,* Mary Sutherland lived in Camberwell. She didn't know Mr. Angel's address.

Lady Frances Carfax wrote every second week to Miss Dobney, her old governess. Miss Dobney lived in Camberwell. When Lady Frances stopped this regular custom, it alerted Holmes that something was amiss.

COLDHARBOUR (COLD HARBOUR) LANE—SW9 After they arrived at Thaddeus Sholto's house in Cold Harbour Lane, he told Holmes, Watson, and Mary Morstan of her father's involvement in *The Sign of Four.*

LARKHALL (LARK HALL) LANE—SW4 In *The Sign of Four,* Thaddeus Sholto sent his driver to bring Miss Morstan from the Lyceum Theatre to Cold Harbour Lane in Lambeth. Holmes and Watson accompanied her. On the way, they drove down Lark Hall Lane.

STOCKWELL ROAD (PLACE)—SW9 In *The Sign of Four,* the coach drove Holmes, Watson, and Miss Morstan from the Lyceum Theatre to Thaddeus Sholto's house in Cold Harbour Lane. The route took them down Stockwell Place.

SOUTH BRIXTON—SW2 In *The Veiled Lodger,* Watson went to Baker Street after receiving a hurried note from Holmes. There, he met Mrs. Merrilow of South Brixton. In the late 19th-century, South Brixton was a popular middle-class suburb.

CANNON STREET UNDERGROUND STATION

CANNON STREET TRAIN STATION—EC4 In *The Twisted Lip,* Neville St. Clair returned home to Kent every evening from the Cannon Street Train Station. He spent his days in the City, begging.

CHANCERY LANE UNDERGROUND STATION

HOLBORN BAR—EC1 Stone obelisks mark the boundary of the City at Holborn. In *The Three Gables,* Steve Dixie, the Negro bruiser, burst into Baker Street to threaten Holmes. When Holmes mentioned the killing of young Perkins outside Holborn Bar, "the Negro's face turned leaden."

Some think that the word "outside" indicates the murder took place outside a public building in the area. I think it simply means outside the City, at Holborn Bar.

CHARING CROSS UNDERGROUND STATION

ADELAIDE STREET—WC2 The Lowther Arcade had its main entrance on The Strand, and its rear exit on Adelaide Street. In *The Final Problem*, Holmes instructed Watson to exit the hansom at the Strand end, dash through the Arcade, and enter the waiting brougham on Adelaide Street. If he followed instructions, he would reach Victoria Station just in time.

AMERICAN EXCHANGE—The Strand, WC2 In *A Study in Scarlet*, a letter in the pocket of Enoch J. Drebber was addressed to the American Exchange, Strand. In the 1890's, the American Exchange office was located in the Strand, next to the Charing Cross Train Station's west entry gate.

CARLTON CLUB—SW1 The Carlton Club was founded in 1832. In 1836, they moved into their Pall Mall building, near the Duke of York's Column. In *The Illustrious Client*, Sir James Damery wrote Holmes from the Carlton Club in Pall Mall. He wanted to consult Holmes on Violet de Merville's infatuation.

CARLTON HOUSE TERRACE (CARLTON TERRACE)—SW1 On the Duke of York's Steps, near the Duke's Column, there are two small doors. One is near, what was once, the German Embassy. In *His Last Bow*, Von Bork was told; "When you get the signal book through the little door…you can put a finis to your record in England."

In *The Priory School*, the Duke of Holdernesse's London residence was in Carlton Terrace.

CHARING CROSS—WC2 In *The Hound of the Baskervilles*, Dr. Mortimer came to London to meet Sir Henry Baskerville, newly arrived from Canada. Sir Henry received a letter at the Northumberland Hotel with the postmark of the Charing Cross Post Office. Holmes wondered how the sender knew that Sir Henry was staying at the Northumberland.

Friends of Dr. Mortimer, at the old Charing Cross Hospital, had given him an engraved walking stick. The Hospital was located in the triangular site where William IV and Agar Streets meet the Strand.

This was also the hospital where Holmes was brought, after he was attacked in *The Illustrious Client.*

On a bleak, windy day, in March 1892, Holmes received a telegram from the Charing Cross telegraph office. It was from Scott Eccles, and read; "HAVE JUST HAD MOST INCREDIBLE AND GROTESQUE EXPERIENCE. MAY I CONSULT YOU?" This started *The Adventure of Wisteria Lodge.*

In *The Abbey Grange,* Holmes sent Inspector Hopkins a telegram from the Charing Cross telegraph office. It advised Hopkins to drag the Abbey Grange Pond. When Hopkins found the silver, he thought Holmes was a wizard.

In *The Greek Interpreter,* Mr. Melas was picked up at his Pall Mall lodgings. The four-wheeler carriage started off through Charing Cross, up Shaftesbury Avenue to Oxford Street. When he commented that this was a roundabout way to Kensington, the windows were covered.

NORTHUMBERLAND AVENUE—WC2 In T*he Illustrious Client,* Watson was walking on Northumberland between the Grand Hotel and Charing Cross Station, when a one-legged newsvendor displayed the headline: MURDEROUS ATTACK UPON SHERLOCK HOLMES. Watson felt a pang of horror.

CHARING CROSS HOTEL—The Strand, WC2 This famous old hotel is located in the heart of Sherlock's London. In *The Bruce-Partington Plans,* a message from Colonel Walter to Hugo Oberstein (in reality dictated by Holmes) named the Hotel as their meeting place.

CHARING CROSS TRAIN STATION—The Strand WC2 In *A Scandal in Bohemia,* Irene Adler and her new husband, Godfrey Norton, left for the Continent on the 5:15 train from Charing Cross Station. They were trying to escape from the King of Bohemia's agents, Holmes included.

In *The Golden Pince-Nez,* Stanley Hopkins, the young detective, arrived at Baker Street late one night. He had just returned by the last train to Charing Cross Station. He asked Holmes and Watson to accompany him back to Yoxley Old Place on the 6AM train.

In response to a letter from Stanley Hopkins, Holmes and Watson left early one morning for a trip to *The Abbey Grange,* in Kent. It wasn't until they had consumed some hot tea in Charing Cross Station, and taken their places on the Kentish train, that they were sufficiently thawed to talk about their journey.

In *The Empty House* we learn that it was in the Charing Cross waiting room, where Holmes had his canine tooth knocked out by Mathews.

In *The Second Stain,* photographs proved conclusively that Henri Fournaye and Eduardo Lucas were one and the same. When Mme. Fournaye arrived from Paris, she attracted much attention at Charing Cross Station.

COCKSPUR STREET—SW1 In *The Abbey Grange,* the shipping office of the Adelaide-Southampton Line was where Pall Mall meets Cockspur Street. Here, Holmes learned of Captain Jack Crocker, and surmised his role in the death of Sir Eustace Brakenstall.

CRAIG'S COURT—SW1 Cox and King's Bank was located in this small court near Charing Cross. In *The Problem of Thor Bridge,* Watson said, "In the vaults of Cox and Co., at Charing Cross, there is a travel-worn and battered tin dispatch box with my name…painted on the lid."

440 THE STRAND—WC2 This was the site of the Lowther Arcade. In *The Final Problem,* Holmes instructed Watson to exit the hansom at the Strand End, dash through the Arcade, and enter the waiting brougham on Adelaide Street. If he followed instructions, he would reach Victoria Station just in time.

PALL MALL—SW1 In *The Greek Interpreter,* Sherlock mentions that his older brother, Mycroft, lived in Pall Mall chambers, with his Diogenes Club just opposite. Melas, the interpreter, had lodgings on the floor above.

GREAT SCOTLAND YARD—SW1 In 1829, the Commissioner of Police set up his office at #4 Whitehall Place. The rear entrance was on Great Scotland Yard, and the picturesque name caught on. When the police headquarters moved in 1891, the name "Scotland Yard" went with it.

THE STRAND—WC2 The Strand was at the center of Sherlock's West End. In *A Study in Scarlet,* Watson recounted that after returning from India, and before meeting Sherlock, he stayed for some time in a private hotel in the Strand.

In *The Red-headed League,* McFarlane's carriage-building depot was in the Strand, next to a Vegetarian Restaurant.

In *The Missing Three-Quarter,* Holmes received a telegram from Cyril Overton. It was sent from the Strand Post Office, and read; "PLEASE AWAIT ME. TERRIBLE MISFORTUNE. RIGHT WING THREEQUAR-TER MISSING, INDISPENSABLE TOMORROW."

In *The Hound of the Baskervilles,* Sir Henry, who had just arrived from Canada, bought a new pair of brown boots in the Strand. He paid six dollars for them, and one was stolen before he had them on his feet.

In *The Resident Patient,* Holmes and Watson grew weary of their Baker Street sitting room. They took a three-hour stroll through the West End, watching the "ebbs and flows through Fleet Street and the Strand."

In *The Sign of Four,* Holmes, Watson, and Miss Morstan took a cab down the Strand toward the Lyceum. It was a damp September evening, and "the lamps were but misty splotches of diffused light."

TRAFALGAR SQUARE—WC2 In *The Hound of the Baskervilles,* John Clayton, the cabby, picked up a passenger at Trafalgar Square. His fare told him that he was Sherlock Holmes. This incident alerted Holmes as to the character of his adversary.

TRAFALGAR SQUARE FOUNTAIN—WC2 In *The Noble Bachelor,* when Lestrade told Holmes that the Serpentine was being dragged for the body of Hatty Doran, Holmes laughed and asked if he was also dragging the Trafalgar Square Fountain. "Because you have just as good a chance of finding this lady in the one as in the other."

CAMDEN TOWN UNDERGROUND STATION

REGENT'S PARK ZOO—NW1 Holmes told Watson that *Charles Augustus Milverton* reminded him of the serpents in the Regent's Park Zoo, "and yet I can't get out of doing business with him."

CLAPHAM COMMON UNDERGROUND STATION

CLAPHAM JUNCTION—SW11 After Mr. Melas, *The Greek Interpreter,* was forced to interpret poor Paul Kratides, he was let out near Clapham Junction. From there, Melas was just in time to catch the last train to Victoria Station.

Colonel Ross, Holmes, and Watson were passing through Clapham Junction, before Holmes had finished explaining how he solved the *Silver Blaze* mystery. Colonel Ross was invited to Baker Street to hear all of the details.

In *The Naval Treaty,* Joseph Harrison drove Holmes and Watson to the train station. There, they caught the Portsmouth train to London. As they passed Clapham Junction, Holmes remarked; "It's a very cheering thing to come into London by any of these lines which run high and allow you to look down on houses like this." Watson thought he was joking.

CLAPHAM NORTH UNDERGROUND STATION

PRIORY GROVE—SW8 In *The Sign of Four,* the cabman driving Holmes, Watson, and Miss Morstan from the Lyceum Theatre to Cold Harbour Lane in Lambeth, passed down Priory Grove.

CLAPHAM SOUTH UNDERGROUND STATION

WANDSWORTH COMMON—SW11 Mr. Melas, *The Greek Interpreter,* who was forced to interpret poor Paul Kratides, was let out in Wandsworth Common. He was just in time to catch the last train from Clapham Junction to Victoria Station.

COVENT GARDEN UNDERGROUND STATION

BOW STREET POLICE COURT—WC2 Founded in 1740, this famous police court was the home of the pre-Scotland Yard policemen. Called the Bow Street Runners, they were paid by the capture, much as bounty hunters are today.

In *The Man with the Twisted Lip,* Inspector Bradstreet was on duty at the Bow Street Station when Holmes and Watson arrived to unmask Hugh Boone. Boone was, in fact, Neville St. Clair, in disguise.

BURLEIGH STREET—WC2 12 Burleigh Street was the location of the new publisher, who introduced Sherlock Holmes to London and the world. The Burleigh Street Magazine was the obvious choice of a name, but *The Strand Magazine* had a better ring to it.

COVENT GARDEN—WC2 In *The Blue Carbuncle,* Breckinridge had a stand in Covent Garden, where he sold geese. The goose he sold Windigate, proprietor of the Alpha Inn, contained the fabulous jewel. Holmes and Watson walked from the Alpha Inn to Covent Garden, "through a zigzag of slums."

ENDELL STREET—WC2 In *The Blue Carbuncle,* Holmes and Watson passed through Endell Street on their way to Covent Garden. They were trying to find out the source of the goose, in which the jewel was found.

LYCEUM THEATRE—WC2 In *The Sign of Four,* Mary Morstan asked Holmes and Watson to accompany her to the Lyceum Theatre. She was following the instructions in a mysterious note she received, which described her as a "wronged woman."

The Lyceum Theatre was closed after several fires in the 19th Century. It re-opened in 1904, and was known for Victorian melodramas. After World War II, the Lyceum was converted to a dance hall, and then closed again for several years before being re-opened in 1996.

ROYAL OPERA HOUSE—Covent Garden, WC2 Completed in 1858, this is London's leading opera house. In *The Adventure of the Red Circle,* Holmes said, "By the way, it is not eight o'clock, and a Wagner night at Covent Garden! If we hurry, we might be in time for the second act."

After the successful conclusion of *The Hound of the Baskervilles,* Holmes reserved a box at the Royal Opera House, to see "Les Huguenots."

STANFORDS (STAMFORD'S)—12/14 Long Acre, WC2 This famous map shop was founded in 1852. In *The Hound of the Baskervilles,* Holmes sent to Stamford's for a large-scale Ordnance map of that part of Devonshire, which included Baskerville Hall.

WELLINGTON and BOW STREETS—WC2 In *The Man with the Twisted Lip,* Holmes and Watson returned from St. Clair's home in Kent. On their way to the Bow Street Police Court, they traveled along Waterloo Bridge Road and Wellington Street.

EDGWARE ROAD UNDERGROUND STATION

EDGWARE ROAD—W2 In *A Scandal in Bohemia,* The Church of St. Monica was in Edgware Road. Here, Godfrey Norton and Irene Adler were married, with a disguised Sherlock as witness.

In *The Three Garridebs,* Holloway and Steele, the house agents for Nathan Garridebs, were located in Edgware Road.

EMBANKMENT UNDERGROUND STATION

CRAVEN STREET—WC2 In *The Illustrious Client,* Watson mentions that he and Holmes had a weakness for the Turkish bath. Theirs was the Charing Cross Turkish Bath. It was located in the wedged shaped building where Craven Street joins Northumberland Avenue.

In *The Hound of the Baskervilles,* Stapleton brought his wife to London and lodged at the Mexborough Private Hotel in Craven Street. He kept her imprisoned in the room, while he followed Dr. Morton to Baker Street, and later, to the Northumberland Hotel.

CRAVEN (NORTHUMBERLAND) PASSAGE—WC2 The women's entrance to the Charing Cross Turkish Bath was through Craven Passage, which in Sherlock's time was called Northumberland Passage. Holmes and Watson's fondness for the Turkish bath was mentioned in *The Illustrious Client.*

IN THE FOOTSTEPS OF SHERLOCK HOLMES—London Walks, Tel: 7624-3978 If you want to go with Holmes and Watson when "The game is afoot", try this afternoon walking tour. It covers the Strand, Covent Garden, and the Sherlock Holmes Pub. The group assembles at the entrance to the Embankment Tube Station at 2:30PM every Thursday. Call in advance to see if the time has changed.

SHERLOCK HOLMES PUB—10/11 Northumberland Street, WC2 For fans of Sherlock Holmes, this is the pub to visit. On the ground level there is a traditional pub. Upstairs they have a restaurant, complete with a glassed-in replica of the 221B Baker Street sitting room. Originally, the building was a small modest hotel. In 1883, the name was changed from The Northumberland Hotel to The Northumberland Arms. Based on Conan Doyle's description, it is very unlikely that this could have been

'The Northumberland Hotel' mentioned in *The Hound of the Baskervilles*.

NORTHUMBERLAND AVENUE—SW1 Between where Great Scotland Yard and Whitehall Place run into the west side of Northumberland Avenue, there is a building that once was the Hotel Metropole.

The Metropole is the most likely candidate for being 'The Northumberland Hotel' in *The Hound of the Baskervilles*. In 1888, Sir Henry was there when he received the warning message, "AS YOU VALUE YOUR LIFE…KEEP AWAY FROM THE MOOR." While at the hotel, he also lost a new brown boot, and then, when it reappeared, an old black boot was taken. This gave Sherlock a clue.

Mr. Melas, *The Greek Interpreter,* acted as a guide to the wealthy Orientals, who stayed at the Northumberland grand hotels.

Many Sherlockian scholars also think that The Metropole was the hotel, at which Francis H. Milton stayed in *The Nobel Bachelor.* Today, the closest "grand" hotel is The Royal Horseguards.

WATERLOO BRIDGE—SE1 In *The Five Orange Pips,* after receiving a threat from the Klu Klux Klan, John Openshaw consulted Holmes. Later, on his way to Waterloo Station, Openshaw was thrown from the Embankment, into the Thames near Waterloo Bridge.

VICTORIA EMBANKMENT—WC2 In *The Five Orange Pips,* John Openshaw was found drowned in the Thames. Holmes wonders how members of the Klu Klux Klan decoyed John Openshaw from Waterloo Bridge to the Embankment.

EUSTON UNDERGROUND STATION

EUSTON TRAIN STATION—NW1 In *A Study in Scarlet,* Drebber and Stangerson were seen on the Euston Station platform, presumably, waiting for the Liverpool Express.

In *The Priory School,* Holmes, Watson, and Dr. Huxtable, left from Euston Station en route to Mackleton.

In T*he Blanched Soldier,* Holmes and James M. Dodd were joined at Euston Station by Sir James Saunders. The three left from here on their journey to Tuxbury Old Park.

EUSTON SQUARE UNDERGROUND STATION

226 GORDON SQUARE—WC1 In *The Noble Bachelor,* Francis Hay Moulton, who married Hatty Doran, lodged at No. 226 Gordon Square.

FARRINGDON UNDERGROUND STATION

FARRINGDON (FARRINGTON) STREET—EC4 In *The Red-headed League,* Holmes, Watson, Inspector Jones, and Mr. Merryweather, drove along Farrington Street on their way to capturing John Clay.

SAFFRON HILL—EC1 In *The Six Napoleons,* Lestrade told Holmes that the Yard had an inspector who made a specialty of the Saffron Hill Italian Quarter. He knew Pietro Venucci on sight, and knew that he was connected with the Mafia.

FULHAM BROADWAY UNDERGROUND STATION

FULHAM ROAD—SW6. In *The Hound of the Baskervilles,* Stapleton bought the hound from Ross & Mangles, dog dealers in Fulham Road.

GLOUCESTER ROAD UNDERGROUND STATION

CORNWALL (CAULFIELD) GARDENS—SW7 In *The Bruce-Partington Plans,* Hugo Oberstein's townhouse was in Caulfield Gardens. It backed up to the aboveground section of the Circle Line, thereby, allowing Cadogan West's body to be placed on the roof of the train.

GLOUCESTER ROAD—SW7 In *The Bruce-Partington Plans,* Holmes asked Watson to meet him at Goldini's Restaurant in Gloucester Road. He told him to bring a revolver and burglar tools. Holmes must have liked Italian food. In another adventure, he mentions Marcini's.

GLOUCESTER ROAD STATION—SW7 In *The Bruce-Partington Plans,* the Circle Line tracks near Gloucester Road Station are clear of tunnels. Herr Oberstein's windows in Caulfield Gardens overlooked the tracks. This gave Holmes a clue.

GOODGE STREET UNDERGROUND STATION

GOODGE STREET and TOTTENHAM COURT ROAD—W1 In *The Blue Carbuncle,* this was the intersection where Henry Baker lost the goose and his hat. He did not know that the Countess of Morcar's jewel was in the goose. After the fracas, Peterson, the commissionaire, ended up with both the hat and the goose.

TOTTENHAM COURT ROAD—WC1 In *The Red Circle,* Mr. Warren was a timekeeper at Morton and Waylight's in Tottenham Court Road.

In *The Cardboard Box* we also learn the Holmes bought his Stradivarius from a Jew broker in Tottenham Court Road.

GREEN PARK UNDERGROUND STATION

BERKELEY (BARCLAY) SQUARE—W1 In *The Illustrious Client,* General de Merville, and his daughter Violet, lived at 104 Berkeley Square.

Admiral Sinclair also lived on the Square in *The Bruce-Partington Plans.* Here, Watson spelled it B-a-r-c-l-a-y, the way it is pronounced.

BOODLE'S—28 St. James's Street, SW1 This gentlemen's club was formed in 1762, and is famous for its bow window, fronting St. James's Street.

In *The Three Gables,* Holmes went to see Langdale Pike, who spent his waking hours in Boodle's bow window, gathering London gossip.

CHRISTIE'S—8 King Street, SW1 This famous auction house was founded in 1766. In *The Illustrious Client,* if pressed for a price, Watson was to suggest that Christie's or Sotheby's set the value of the blue Ming saucer.

In *The Three Garridebs,* Nathan Garrideb lived in an abode of Bohemian bachelors. He rarely left his quarters, except to go to Christie's to bid on additions to his natural history collection.

CURZON STREET—W1 In *Shoscombe Old Place* we learn that Sam Brewer, the well-known moneylender, lived on Curzon Street. Sir Robert Norberton nearly horsewhipped Brewer to death on Newmarket Heath.

HALF MOON STREET—W1 In *The Illustrious Client,* Watson, under his alias Dr. Hill Barton, supposedly lived at No. 369 Half Moon Street. As Barton, he went to see Baron Gruner about the blue Ming saucer.

MUSEUM OF MANKIND (former University of London)—Burlington Gardens, W1 In *A Study in Scarlet,* we find that Watson received his medical degree from The University of London. At that time, the University was located in Burlington Gardens, where the Museum of Mankind is now located.

In *The Resident Patient,* Dr. Percy Trevelyan was also a medical graduate of the University of London.

ST. JAMES'S STREET—SW1 In *The Greek Interpreter,* Holmes and Watson walked to Mycroft's club in Pall Mall. Since they entered Pall Mall from the St. James's Street end, they must have walked past Boodle's, where Langdale Pike spent his waking hours in the bow window.

GREENWICH UNDERGROUND STATION

BLACKHEATH—SE12 In *The Norwood Builder*, in an attempt to help the unfortunate John Hector McFarlane, Holmes and Watson first went towards Blackheath.

In *The Sussex Vampire*, we learn that in his younger days, Watson played rugby for the Blackheath Club. Robert Ferguson, who played for Richmond, remembered the day he threw Watson into the crowd at the Old Deer Park.

In *The Retired Colourman*, Watson took the train from Blackheath to Lewisham to visit The Haven, Josiah Amberley's home.

Cyril Overton called on Holmes to seek his help in finding *The Missing Three-Quarter*. Overton was amazed that Holmes had never heard of Godfrey Staunton, the three-quarter who played rugby for Cambridge and Blackheath.

In *The Engineer's Thumb*, Mr. Victor Hatherley had been apprenticed to Venner & Matheson, the well-known engineering firm in Greenwich. Later he went into business for himself, but got into a situation that resulted in the loss of his thumb.

HAMMERSMITH UNDERGROUND STATION

HAMMERSMITH—W6 In *The Second Stain*, Mitton, Eduardo Lucas's valet, was out the night of the murder, visiting a friend in Hammersmith.

In *The Sussex Vampire*, while Holmes looked in his great index volume under "V," he found; Victor Lynch the forger, Vittoria the circus belle, and Vigor, the Hammersmith wonder.

HAMMERSMITH BRIDGE—W6 Holmes made a pact with Lestrade in *The Six Napoleons*, "If you come with me to Chiswick tonight…I promise to go to the Italian Quarter with you tomorrow." Later that night, the four-wheeler dropped them near Hammersmith Bridge.

CHISWICK—W6 The four-wheeler was at their door at eleven, as Holmes and Watson left for 'Laburnum Villa in Chiswick. There, with the help of the owner, Mr. Josiah Brown, they solved the case of *The Six Napoleons.*

HAMPSTEAD UNDERGROUND STATION

CHURCH ROW—NW3 On the night they went to burgle *Charles Augustus Milverton*'s house, Holmes and Watson took a cab as far as Church Row in Hampstead.

HAMPSTEAD—NW3 In *The Valley of Fear,* Cecil James Barker lived in Hales Lodge, Hampstead. He lied to the police to help his friend John Douglas, who was later killed by Moriarty.

In *The Stock-Broker's Clerk,* Hall Pycroft lived at No. 17 Potter's Terrace in Hampstead.

Charles Augustus Milverton, who Holmes called "the worst man in London," lived in Appledore Towers, Hampstead. One splendid night, Holmes and Watson went to Hampstead to burgle Milverton's house.

HAMPSTEAD HEATH—NW3 In *The Red Circle,* Mrs. Warren didn't know what to make of the strange behavior of her lodger. She reached her limit when her husband, a timekeeper at Morton and Waylight's in Tottenham Court Road, was abducted and dropped off on Hampstead Heath.

HARROW AND WEALDSTONE UNDERGROUND STATION

HARROW WEALD—HA1 Mary Maberley asked Holmes to visit her house, *Three Gables* at Harrow Weald. She had received a very strange offer to buy the house and its contents. Later, the Barney Stockdale Gang burgled the house.

HIGH STREET KENSINGTON UNDERGROUND STATION

CHURCH STREET—W8 In *The Empty House,* an old bibliophile claimed to be a neighbor of Watson's (in Kensington). The old man said he had a little bookstore at the corner of Church Street. Watson almost fainted when he turned around and found that the old man was really Holmes in disguise.

KENSINGTON HIGH STREET—W8 In *The Six Napoleons,* Harding Brothers had a shop on the High Street. They bought three plaster busts of Napoleon, from Gelder and Co., and sold them to Harker, Brown, and Sandeford.

131 PITT STREET—W8 In *The Six Napoleons,* Mr. Horace Harker of the Central Press Association lived at No. 131 Pitt Street, Kensington. He bought a bust of Napoleon from Harding Brothers. It was stolen, and a man was murdered on his doorstep.

HOLBORN UNDERGROUND STATION

FLEET STREET—EC4 In *The Resident Patient,* Holmes and Watson grew weary of their Baker Street sitting room. They took a three-hour stroll through the West End, watching the "ebbs and flows through Fleet Street and the Strand."

In *The Bruce-Partington Plans,* Holmes and Watson went to the Fleet Street district to place a newspaper advertisement. It read: "TO-NIGHT. SAME HOUR. SAME PLACE. TWO TAPS. MOST VITALLY IMPORTANT. YOUR SAFETY AT STAKE. PIERROT."

HIGH HOLBORN—WC1 It was a cold evening when Holmes, Watson, and Inspector Baynes, set off for *Wisteria Lodge.* The place was empty, but there was a great deal of clothing, with the stamp of Marx and Co., High Holborn.

MONTAGUE STREET—WC1 In *The Musgrave Ritual,* Holmes mentions that he had rooms in Montague Street when he first came to London. He spent his time in The British Museum reading room, studying the sciences that would later make him so efficient.

ROYAL COLLEGE OF SURGEONS—35/43 Lincoln's Inn Fields, WC2
In *The Hound of the Baskervilles,* Dr. Mortimer spent the afternoon at the Museum of the College of Surgeons. He went without Sir Henry.

ISLAND GARDENS STATION (DOCKLANDS LIGHT RR)

ISLE OF DOGS—E14 In *The Sign of Four,* Holmes and Watson attempted to catch the Aurora, "the fastest boat on the river". They shot through the Pool of London in their police steam launch, past the Isle of Dogs.

KENNINGTON UNDERGROUND STATION

KENNINGTON ROAD—SE11 In *The Disappearance of Lady Frances Carfax,* Stimson and Co., the undertaker in Kennington Road, made the "out of the ordinary" casket for the evil Dr. Shlessinger and his wife. It was deep enough for two bodies.

In *The Six Napoleons,* Dr. Barnicot, an admirer of Napoleon, bought two plaster busts from Morse Hudson, who had a shop in Kennington Road. Later, both busts were smashed, one in Barnicot's Kennington Road office.

KNIGHT'S WALK (PLACE)—SW11 In *The Sign of Four,* after following Toby's nose, Holmes and Watson had to make a choice at Knight's Place. Here, the trail split in two different directions. At first, they made followed the wrong trail.

KILBURN UNDERGROUND STATION

KILBURN HIGH ROAD—NW6 In *The Blue Carbuncle,* James Ryder, Head Attendant at the Hotel Cosmopolitan, heard from his crooked friend, Maudsley, how thieves could dispose of stolen property. Maudsley lived in Kilburn.

KING'S CROSS/ST. PANCRAS UNDERGROUND STATION

KING'S CROSS—WC1 In *A Case of Identity*, Mary Sutherland's stepfather, disguised as Hosmer Angel, romanced poor Mary. He was trying to keep her money at home. Mary planned to marry Hosmer at St. Saviour's Church, near King's Cross.

KING'S CROSS RAIL STATION—N1 In *The Missing Three-Quarter*, Holmes and Watson left from King's Cross Station, on their way to Cambridge.

MIDLAND GRAND (ST. PANCRAS) HOTEL—2 St Chad Street, WC1 In *A Case of Identity*, Mary Sutherland had planned her wedding breakfast at the St. Pancras Hotel. It is one of the grand railroad hotels built in the 1860–70s. Today, it is called the Midland Grand Hotel.

LANCASTER GATE UNDERGROUND STATION

LANCASTER GATE—W2 In *The Noble Bachelor*, Aloysius Doran, the wealthy American, took a furnished house in Lancaster Gate. His only daughter was to marry Lord Robert St. Simon. During the wedding breakfast, Hatty disappeared.

LIMEHOUSE UNDERGROUND STATION

RATCLIFF STREET AND THE HIGHWAY (RATCLIFF HIGHWAY)— E1 In *Black Peter*, Holmes asked Watson to send a telegram for him. It read, "SUMNER, SHIPPING AGENT, RATCLIFF HIGHWAY. SEND THREE MEN ON, TO ARRIVE TEN TOMORROW MORNING.— BASIL." Holmes said that Basil was his name in those parts.

LIVERPOOL STREET UNDERGROUND STATION

LIVERPOOL TRAIN STATION—EC2 In *The Dancing Men,* Holmes asked Watson to remain at Baker Street. Hilton Cubitt was to have reached Liverpool Station at one-twenty, and might arrive at any moment.

In *The Retired Colourman,* Watson found that he and Josiah Amberley could take the 5:20 train from Liverpool Station to Little Purlington. Once Amberley found the trip was a wild goose chase, the ploy would require them to wait until the next day, to return.

MANSION HOUSE UNDERGROUND STATION

PAUL'S WALK (PAUL'S WHARF)—EC4 In *The Man with the Twisted Lip,* Holmes said he had located an opium den in Upper Swandam Lane, near Paul's Wharf.

UPPER THAMES STREET (UPPER SWANDAM LANE)—EC4 This is the infamous Lane mentioned in *The Man with the Twisted Lip.* Holmes said, "There is a trap-door at the back of the building…which could tell some strange tales."

MARBLE ARCH UNDERGROUND STATION

HYDE PARK—W2 In *The Red-headed League,* Watson walked from his house in Kensington, through Hyde Park, to Baker Street.

In *The Yellow Face,* Holmes and Watson took an early spring walk in the Park, and found that they had missed a client. Their walk could have been through Regent's Park, but Hyde Park is more likely.

In *The Noble Bachelor,* the missing bride, Hatty Doran St. Simon, was seen walking in Hyde Park with Flora Millar. Flora had been on a "very friendly footing" with Lord St. Simon, and had created a disturbance at the wedding breakfast. In a futile effort to find Hatty, Inspector Lestrade started dragging the Serpentine.

PARK LANE—W1 In *The Empty House,* Ronald Adair, second son of the Earl of Maynooth, lived at No. 427 Park Lane (old numbering), with his mother and sister. He played cards with, and was later murdered by, Colonel Sebastian Moran. Holmes thought that Adair had caught Moran cheating. Later, Watson strolled from Hyde Park, by the site of the murder. He bumped against an elderly bibliophile carrying several books. Although he didn't know it at the time, it was Holmes in disguise.

MONUMENT UNDERGROUND STATION

LIME STREET—EC3 This ancient street in the City was named for the sellers of limes who once congregated there. In *The Mazarin Stone,* Count Sylvius said he would have to go to Lime Street to give the stone to Van Seddar, who had to leave on the next boat.

LONDON BRIDGE—EC4 In *The Bruce-Partington Plans,* Holmes sent his brother a telegram from London Bridge. It read: "SEE SOME LIGHT IN THE DARKNESS, BUT IT MAY POSSIBLY FLICKER OUT. MEAN-WHILE, PLEASE SEND…A COMPLETE LIST OF ALL FOREIGN SPIES (IN ENGLAND)."

MOORGATE UNDERGROUND STATION

DRAPER'S GARDEN—EC2 In *The Stock-Broker's Clerk,* Hall Pycroft had a billet at Coxon and Woodhouse's of Draper's Garden. After the problem with the Venezuelan loan, he and the other twenty-six clerks were let go.

NOTTING HILL GATE UNDERGROUND STATION

LADBROKE GROVE (LOWER BURKE STREET)—W11 Although the name was modified, Ladbroke Grove fits the location of Lower Burke Street. This is where Culverton Smith rented a house "in the vague borderland between Notting Hill and Kensington." In *The Dying Detective,* Smith was a well-known resident of Sumatra, and an expert on oriental diseases.

CAMPDEN HILL (CAMPDEN HOUSE) ROAD—W8 In *The Six Napoleons,* Campden House Road is where Lestrade said one of the Napoleon busts had been found. It had been broken into fragments, in the front garden.

NOTTING HILL—W11 In *The Bruce-Partington Plans,* Mycroft sent Holmes a list of the biggest international spies in London: "Adolph Meyer of 13 Great George Street, Louis La Rothière of Campden Mansions, Notting Hill, and Hugo Oberstein, 13 Caulfield Gardens, Kensington."

OLYMPIA UNDERGROUND STATION

OLYMPIA—W14 In *His Last Bow,* Von Bork was the ideal German agent for Great Britain. He was a sportsman, competing with the British aristocracy in sailing, hunting, and polo. He even matched them by taking a prize in The Horse of the Year Show at Olympia.

OVAL UNDERGROUND STATION

BRIXTON ROAD—SW9 In *A Study in Scarlet,* Holmes placed an advertisement in the "Found" column of every morning paper. It read, "In Brixton Road, this morning, a plain gold wedding band…Apply Dr. Watson, 221B, Baker Street, between eight and nine this evening."

KENNINGTON LANE—SE11 In *The Sign of Four,* Toby led Holmes and Watson in Kennington Lane, just east of the Oval.

'WHITE HART TAVERN' BRIXTON AND CRANMER ROADS—SW9 In *A Study in Scarlet,* Holmes placed an advertisement in the "Found" column of every morning paper. It read, "In Brixton Road…a plain gold wedding band, found in the roadway between the White Hart Tavern and Holland Grove." Based on this, the White Hart Tavern had to be on the corner of Brixton and Cranmer Roads.

OXFORD CIRCUS UNDERGROUND STATION

CAVENDISH SQUARE—W1 In *The Resident Patient,* Percy Trevelyan revealed that a medical specialist, who aims high, must start in one of a dozen streets in the Cavendish Square quarter. This is still true today.

In *The Empty House,* Holmes stopped the cab at Cavendish Square, as he did at every subsequent street corner, to make sure that he and Watson were not being followed.

CONDUIT STREET—W1 In *The Empty House,* we learn that Colonel Sebastian Moran, who lived in Conduit Street, was the second most dangerous man in London.

LANGHAM HOTEL—Portland Place, W1 During Holmes's time, the fact that you were a guest at the Langham automatically marked you as a gentleman. In *A Scandal in Bohemia,* the King of Bohemia, under the pseudonym Count Von Kramm, stayed there.

In *The Sign of Four,* Captain Morstan telegraphed his daughter, Mary, to meet him at the Langham. When she arrived, he was missing.

The Hon. Philip Green, the son of a famous admiral of the same name, stayed at the Langham in *The Disappearance of Lady Frances Carfax.*

MORTIMER STREET—W1 In *The Final Problem,* Watson was married and in private practice. He lived in a house that backed up to Mortimer Street. Holmes visited him there as they made plans to elude Professor Moriarty. As he left, Holmes clambered over the back wall, into Mortimer Street.

OXFORD STREET—W1 In *The Greek Interpreter,* Holmes and Watson walked along Oxford Street toward Regent Circus. They were on their way to Mycroft Holmes's club in Pall Mall. They must have turned south before they reached the Circus, because they reached Pall Mall from the St. James's Street end.

OXFORD (REGENT) CIRCUS—W1 After the murder of *Charles Augustus Milverton*, Holmes and Watson hurried down Oxford Street to a shop near Regent (Oxford) Circus. There, in the window, they saw a picture of a regal lady in court dress. Holmes put his finger to his lips, indicating that they must keep the secret.

ST GEORGE'S HANOVER SQUARE—2a Mill Street, W1 In *The Noble Bachelor*, St George's was the church in which Lord Robert St Simon, second son of the Duke of Balmoral, was to marry Miss Hatty Doran, daughter of a California millionaire.

WIGMORE STREET—W1 In *The Adventure of the Blue Carbuncle*, Holmes and Watson walked along Wigmore Street on their way from Baker Street to The Alpha Inn. "Our footfalls rang out crisply and loudly as we swung through the doctors' quarter; Wimpole Street, Harley Street, and through Wigmore Street into Oxford Street. In a quarter of an hour, we were in Bloomsbury at the Alpha Inn."

In *The Sign of Four*, Holmes demonstrated the power of deduction by observing that Watson had been to the Wigmore Post Office, and while there, had dispatched a telegram. As usual, Watson was amazed.

PADDINGTON UNDERGROUND STATION

PADDINGTON DISTRICT—W2 In *The Stock-Broker's Clerk*, we learn that shortly after his marriage, Watson bought a medical practice in the Paddington district.

PADDINGTON TRAIN STATION—W2 Watson and his wife were having breakfast one morning, when he received a telegram from Holmes. It read; "HAVE YOU A COUPLE OF DAYS TO SPARE?…LEAVE PADDINGTON BY THE 1:15." This started the case of *The Boscombe Valley Mystery*. When Watson arrived at the station, "Holmes was pacing up and down the platform, his tall gaunt figure made even gaunter and taller by his long grey traveling-cloak and the close fitting cloth cap."

In the summer of 1889, Victor Hatherley, a hydraulic engineer, departed from Paddington Train Station to meet Colonel Lysander Stark near Reading. That misadventure resulted in the loss of Hatherley's thumb. Later, Watson's maid woke him up to announce that two men had just arrived from Paddington Station, and that one of them needed medical attention. This started *The Adventure of the Engineer's Thumb.*

In *Silver Blaze,* Holmes and Watson left from the Paddington Rail Station on their way to King's Pyland in Dartmoor. By timing the telegraph poles, which were placed sixty yards apart, Holmes calculated that the train was traveling at fifty-three and a half miles per hour.

Paddington was also the train station from which Watson, Dr. Mortimer, and Sir Henry left London on their way to Baskerville Hall. They did not know what awaited them in *The Hound of the Baskervilles.*

PICCADILLY CIRCUS UNDERGROUND STATION

CAFE ROYAL—68 Regent Street, W1 In *The Illustrious Client,* Holmes was attacked in Piccadilly Circus. He escaped by running through the Café Royal. The restaurant is still there, and an excellent place to dine.

CRITERION BAR—222 Piccadilly, W1 Immortalized in *A Study in Scarlet,* the Criterion has reopened. The restaurant, and its famous long bar, is again the place to meet. It was here that Watson met young Stamford. When Stamford found out that Watson was looking for someone to go halves on lodging, he reluctantly mentioned Holmes.

GLASSHOUSE STREET—W1 In *The Illustrious Client,* the men who attacked Holmes were respectably dressed. Holmes escaped by running through the Café Royal, into Glasshouse Street.

PICCADILLY—SW1 In the 1890s, St. James's Hall, Piccadilly, was London's leading concert hall. In *The Red-headed League,* Holmes and Watson spent one afternoon listening to the Spanish violinist, Pablo Sarasate; play at St. James's.

REGENT STREET—W1 In *The Hound of the Baskervilles,* Holmes and Watson followed Sir Henry along Regent Street, and noticed there was another follower in a hansom cab. After the hansom cab sped away, Holmes enlisted the help of young Cartwright, who worked in the Regent Street's district messenger service office. He was told to go to each of the twenty-three hotels in the Charing Cross area, to see if he could find a clue.

In Scandal in Bohemia, Godfrey Norton rushed into Gross and Hankey's in Regent Street.

SHAFTESBURY AVENUE—W1 In *The Greek Interpreter,* Mr. Melas was picked up at his Pall Mall lodgings. The carriage started off through Charing Cross, up Shaftesbury Avenue to Oxford Street. When he commented that this was a roundabout way to Kensington, they covered the windows.

ST. JAMES'S SQUARE—SW1 The London Library is still located in St. James's Square. Thomas Carlyle, the historian, founded it in 1841, as an alternative to the library at the British Museum. In *The Adventure of the Illustrious Client,* Watson needed twenty-four hours of intensive study to pose as an expert on Chinese pottery. His friend Lomax, the Sub-Librarian, helped him find books for the task.

THEATRE ROYAL, HAYMARKET—Haymarket Street, SW1 In *The Retired Colourman,* Josiah Amberley had taken two upper circle seats at the Haymarket Theatre. He said he went alone because his wife had a headache.

PIMLICO UNDERGROUND STATION

MILLBANK—SW1 In *The Sign of Four,* Holmes and Watson took a wherry from Mordecai Smith's boat yard to Millbank, on the north side of the river.

VAUXHALL BRIDGE ROAD—SW1 In *The Sign of Four,* Holmes, Watson, and Mary Morstan, were driven to see Thaddeus Sholto. They came down Vauxhall Bridge Road and crossed the river.

VINCENT SQUARE—SW1 In *The Sign of Four,* before turning on Vauxhall Bridge Road, Holmes, Watson, and Mary Morstan, drove down Rochester Row and saw Vincent Square on their left.

PUTNEY BRIDGE UNDERGROUND STATION

HURLINGHAM PARK—SW6 After accepting Sir James Damery's commission from *The Illustrious Client,* Watson mused about what else was known about Baron Gruner. "He has expensive tastes. He is a horse fancier, and for a short time played polo at Hurlingham."

REGENT'S PARK UNDERGROUND STATION

HARLEY STREET—W1 Harley Street is the location for well-placed West End physicians. Doctor Moore Agar, of #6 Harley Street, advised Holmes to take a country rest or suffer a complete breakdown. Holmes and Watson went to Cornwall, and found *The Devil's Foot.*

In *The Blue Carbuncle,* Holmes and Watson walked past Harley Street on their way from Baker Street to the Alpha Inn (Museum Tavern?).

In *The Resident Patient,* Holmes and Watson walked back home from Percy Trevelyan office on Brook Street. They "had crossed Oxford Street and were halfway down Harley Street" before Watson could get a word out of Holmes.

RICHMOND UNDERGROUND STATION

RICHMOND—SW14 In *The Sussex Vampire,* Robert Ferguson had played rugby for Richmond in his younger days. He recognized Watson as someone he had played against.

OLD DEER PARK—Richmond SW14 In *The Sussex Vampire* we learn that when he was younger, Watson had played rugby for the Blackheath Club. Ferguson remembered the day he threw Watson into the crowd at the Old Deer Park.

ROTHERHITHE UNDERGROUND STATION

ROTHERHITHE—SE18 In Victorian times, this dockside area, across the Thames from Wapping, was a very rough place. In *The Dying Detective,* Holmes, supposedly, picked up a coolie disease in Rotherhithe, and returned to Baker Street to die.

RUSSELL SQUARE UNDERGROUND STATION

GREAT ORMOND (ORME) STREET—WC1 In *The Red Circle,* the Warrens lived on Great Orme Street. Mrs. Warren consulted Holmes about her lodger, who was really Emilia Lucca, although no one knew it at the time.

RUSSELL SQUARE—WC1 When he came up to London for the Jubilee, Hilton Cubitt stayed in a boardinghouse in Russell Square. There he met the American, Elsie Parker. After their marriage, Elsie started receiving *The Dancing Men* messages.

SHADWELL UNDERGROUND STATION

CHRISTIAN (CHURCH) STREET—E1 Called Church Street in *The Six Napoleons,* this street, in Stepney, is where the firm of Gelder and Co. was located. They were a well-known house in the trade, and made the busts of Napoleon. Holmes knew that Beppo was the common factor.

SOUTH KENSINGTON UNDERGROUND STATION

THE ALBERT HALL—Kensington, SW7 In *The Retired Colourman,* Holmes felt that he and Watson should dress, dine, and go hear Carina sing at the Albert Hall.

ST JAMES'S PARK UNDERGROUND STATION

GREAT PETER STREET—SW1 In *The Sign of Four,* Holmes wired from the Great Peter Street Post Office, to the Baker Street Division of the detective police force.

ROCHESTER ROW—SW1 In *The Sign of Four,* the coachman who met Holmes, Watson, and Miss Morstan at the Lyceum, drove them along Rochester Row on their way to Lambeth.

TOTHILL STREET—SW1 The old Imperial Theatre was part of an amusement complex known as the Royal Aquarium. It covered the site now occupied by the Wesleyan Central Hall, on the north side of Tothill Street. In *The Solitary Cyclist,* Violet Smith's late father, "conducted the orchestra at the old Imperial Theatre."

ST JOHN'S WOOD UNDERGROUND STATION

ST. JOHN'S WOOD—NW8 In *A Scandal in Bohemia,* Irene Adler lived in Briony Lodge, St. John's Wood. Holmes devised a scheme to find out where she hid the picture of her and the King of Bohemia.

ST PAUL'S UNDERGROUND STATION

GRESHAM HOUSE, HOLBORN VIADUCT—EC1 In *The Norwood Builder,* the unhappy John Hector McFarlane was a junior partner in Graham and McFarlane of 426 Gresham Buildings.

KING EDWARD STREET—EC1 Jabez Wilson went to the offices of *The Red-headed League* to do his daily task, and found the door locked. He was told that Duncan Ross, who was really solicitor William Morris, had moved to new offices at 17 King Edward Street, near St Paul's.

ST. BARTHOLOMEW'S HOSPITAL—EC1 "St. Bart's", as it is called, is where, in 1881, young Stamford introduced Watson to Holmes. This famous meeting in the chemical laboratory was described in *A Study in Scarlet.*

TEMPLE UNDERGROUND STATION

INNER TEMPLE—EC4 In *A Scandal in Bohemia,* Godfrey Norton practiced law in the Inner Temple. He married Irene Adler, and the two fled to the Continent. When Sherlock later referred to Irene Adler, or looked at her photograph, he always used the honorable title of "The Woman."

SIMPSON'S IN THE STRAND—100 Strand, WC2 Simpson's, arguable the best-known English restaurant in London, hasn't changed much since the 1890's. After his three day fast in *The Dying Detective,* Holmes told Watson, "Something nutritious at Simpson's would not be out of place."

In *The Illustrious Client,* Holmes turned to Shinwell Johnson to gain access to his underworld contacts. Watson joined Holmes at Simpson's, where he sat at a table in the front window. Holmes said: "Johnson is on the prowl."

SOMERSET HOUSE—Strand, WC2 In 1883 Somerset House contained the National Archives of Wills. While investigating the case of *The Speckled Band,* Sherlock Holmes went there to examine the will of the Stoner sisters' mother. Holmes used the term "Doctors' Common," which was the ancient ecclesiastical court that had kept such records. Although the function had transferred years before, the term remained in common usage.

TOOTING BEC UNDERGROUND STATION

STREATHAM—SW16 In *The Beryl Coronet,* Alexander Holder, partner in the private banking firm of Holder and Stevenson, took the precious security to his house in Streatham for safekeeping.

TOTTENHAM COURT ROAD UNDERGROUND STATION

BRITISH MUSEUM—Great Russell Street, WC1 The Museum's famous Reading Room contains an enormous collection of scientific works. In *The Musgrave Ritual,* we learn that this is where young Sherlock studied those branches of science that would later make him so efficient.

In *The Hound of the Baskervilles,* the Vandeleurs established a school in Yorkshire. When it failed, they changed their names to Stapleton, and moved to the South of England. Holmes learned that the British Museum considered Stapleton a recognized authority in entomology.

In *Wisteria Lodge,* Holmes visited the British Museum reading up on Eckermann's "Voodooism and the Negroid Religions."

MUSEUM TAVERN (ALPHA INN)—49 Great Russell Street, WC1 This old tavern is the most likely candidate for being the Alpha Inn in *The Blue Carbuncle.* There, some of the regulars, including Henry Baker, joined the Christmas goose club. This started the whole affair.

TOWER HILL UNDERGROUND STATION

MINORIES—EC3 In *The Mazarin Stone,* Holmes followed Count Negretto Sylvius to old Straubenzee's workshop in the Minories. Straubenzee made the air gun that Holmes thought was pointed at him from the window on the other side of Baker Street. Holmes had a target dummy made in his likeness.

VAUXHALL UNDERGROUND STATION

BLACK PRINCE ROAD (PRINCE'S STREET)—SW8 In *The Sign of Four,* Toby led Holmes and Watson through Belmont Place, and Prince's Street, to Broad Street.

BLACK PRINCE ROAD (BROAD STREET)—SW8 In Victorian times, the lower part of Black Prince Road, running down to the Thames, was called Broad Street. In *The Sign of Four,* Toby led Holmes and Watson to Broad Street. The quarry had taken a boat there.

BONDWAY (BOND STREET)—SE8 In *The Sign of Four,* Toby led Holmes and Watson along Kennington Lane, through Bond Street and Miles Street. As they neared the river, Toby stopped and began to run forwards and backwards. He had lost the scent.

KENNINGTON OVAL—SE11 In *The Sign of Four,* Holmes and Watson found themselves in Kennington Lane, to the east of the Oval. After reaching a dead end, Toby "waddled around in circles…as if to ask for sympathy in his embarrassment."

MILES STREET—SE11 In *The Sign of Four,* Toby finally led Holmes and Watson along Miles Street, near the river. Toby stopped and began to run forwards and backwards. He had lost the scent.

NINE ELMS—SW8 In *The Sign of Four,* after pushing the creosote soaked handkerchief under Toby's nose, Holmes, Watson, and the dog followed the wrong trail along Miles Street, to the timber-yard at Nine Elms.

VAUXHALL BRIDGE—SE11 In *The Sign of Four,* Holmes, Watson, and Miss Morstan were driven for a meeting with Thaddeus Sholto in Lambeth. As they crossed the Thames, Holmes remarked that he could catch glimpses of the river.

WANDSWORTH (WORDSWORTH) ROAD—SW8 On the Lambeth side of the river, the coachman turned right on Wordsworth Road. In

The Sign of Four, he was delivering Holmes, Watson, and Miss Morstan to Thaddeus Sholto's house in Lambeth.

VICTORIA UNDERGROUND STATION

VICTORIA TRAIN STATION—SW1 After Mr. Melas, *The Greek Interpreter,* was let out near Clapham Junction, he was just in time to catch the last train to Victoria Station.

In *The Final Problem,* Watson followed Holmes's instructions to the letter. He arrived at the Victoria Train Station just in time to catch the Continental express. Moriarty was close behind.

In *The Valley of Fear,* Inspector McDonald, Holmes, and Watson left from the Victoria Train Station to solve the murder of John Douglas of Birlstone Manor House.

In *The Sussex Vampire,* Robert Ferguson was relieved when Holmes and Watson agreed to take the 2PM train from Victoria to Lamberley in Sussex.

After solving the *Silver Blaze* mystery, Holmes, Watson, and Colonel Ross returned to London at Victoria Station. Holmes invited Colonel Ross to Baker Street for a cigar, and offered to answer all of his questions.

GROSVENOR HOTEL—SW1 In *The Final Problem,* Holmes and Watson reached the little Alpine village of Meiringen. There, they stayed at the Englischer Hof, owned by Peter Steiler, the elder. He spoke excellent English, having served more than three years as waiter at the Grosvenor Hotel in London.

VICTORIA STREET—SW1 In *The Engineer's Thumb,* Victor Hatherley, an engineer, lived in a third floor walk-up at 16A Victoria Street. When he lost his thumb, Watson treated him and took him to consult with Holmes.

WATERLOO UNDERGROUND STATION

WATERLOO BRIDGE ROAD—SE1 In *The Man with the Twisted Lip,* Holmes and Watson returned to London from Neville St. Clair's home in Kent. They traveled down Waterloo Bridge Road, up Wellington Street, to the Bow Street Police Court.

WATERLOO ROAD—SE1 In *The Three Garridebs,* Holmes discovered that John Garrideb was in fact Killer Evens, an American with a sinister and murderous reputation. He came to London in 1893, and shot a man over cards in a nightclub in Waterloo Road in January 1895.

WATERLOO TRAIN STATION—SE1 In *The Speckled Band,* Helen Stoner left Leatherhead on the first train to Waterloo Station. She wanted to consult Holmes on the mysterious death of her twin sister. Later, Holmes and Watson took the route back, to visit Stoke Moran in Surrey.

In *The Naval Treaty,* Holmes and Watson were able to catch an early train from Waterloo to Woking. They were answering a plea for help from Percy Phelps, Watson's old school chum.

In *The Solitary Cyclist,* Watson caught the 9:13 train from Waterloo Station. He wanted to be in place when Violet Smith arrived in Farnham on the 9:50. He wanted to see if the bearded cyclist followed her again.

In *The Hound of the Baskervilles,* Sir Henry Baskerville arrived in London at the Waterloo Rail Station. Dr. Mortimer met him. Later, in trying to find out who was following Sir Henry and Dr. Mortimer, Holmes located the cabman John Clayton. He worked out of Shipley's Yard, near Waterloo Station. His fare had told him that he was Sherlock Holmes. When Holmes heard this, he burst into a hearty laugh.

WEST INDIA QUAY UNDERGROUND STATION

WEST INDIA DOCKS—E14 In *The Sign of Four,* Holmes and Watson attempted to catch the Aurora, "the fastest boat on the river." Their police steam launch shot through the Pool of London, past the West India Docks.

WESTMINSTER UNDERGROUND STATION

THE ADMIRALTY, WHITEHALL—SW1 The Old Admiralty Offices at Whitehall are where it was set down that *The" Gloria Scott"* was lost at sea. No word ever leaked, as to her true fate.

With the death of Arthur Cadogan West, and the missing *Bruce-Partington Plans,* the Admiralty was buzzing like an overturned beehive. Mycroft had never seen the Prime Minister so upset.

In *His Last Bow,* Baron Von Herling complained that The Admiralty had received an alarm on the Naval Signals he had accumulated, and had changed every code.

In The Priory School, the Duke of Holdernesse had been Lord of the Admiralty, with offices at Whitehall.

DOWNING STREET—SW1 In *The Naval Treaty,* Lord Holdhurst, uncle of Percy Phelps, had chambers in Downing Street. Holmes was able to find the missing treaty, and save the honor of poor Percy.

10 DOWNING STREET—SW1 In *The Second Stain,* it was from No. 10 that Lord Bellinger, came to Baker Street to ask Sherlock's help in recovering a missing document of vital importance. The Right Honorable Trelawney Hope, Secretary for European Affairs, who had discovered the loss that very morning, accompanied the Prime Minister.

No. 10 must have also been the place from which another Prime Minister, (or perhaps the same one), came to consult Holmes in *The Mazarin Stone.*

RICHMOND (WHITEHALL) TERRACE—SW1 In my opinion, this was the site of the townhouse occupied by the Right Honorable Trelawney Hope, Secretary for European Affairs, and his wife Lady

Hilda. In *The Second Stain*, the Prime Minister left his busy schedule to come to Hope's house for lunch. The location had to be very close to No. 10 Downing Street. Did they walk, or arrive by carriage?

HOUSES OF PARLIAMENT—SW1 In *The Musgrave Ritual*, Reginald Musgrave visited Holmes at his room in Montague Street. Musgrave said that his father had died, and that in addition to now having to manage the estate, he was a Member of Parliament.

KING CHARLES STREET—SW1 In *The Naval Treaty*, Percy Phelps' office was in the Foreign Office in Whitehall. Whoever stole the treaty, entered and left the building through the side door in King Charles Street.

LITTLE GEORGE STREET—SW1 In *A Study in Scarlet*, Joseph Stangerson's body was discovered in Halliday's Private Hotel in Little George Street. Written above the body, in letters of blood, was written the word RACHE.

NEW SCOTLAND YARD, DERBY GATE—SW1 New Scotland Yard (now closed) opened in 1891 near Westminster Bridge. It figured prominently in many of Sherlock Holmes's cases. Here, in their Black Museum, they kept the air gun that Colonel Moran was going to use, to kill Holmes from *The Empty House*.

WESTMINSTER STAIRS (below Westminster Bridge)—SW1 In *The Sign of Four*, Holmes told Inspector Jones that he needed a fast police steam launch at the Westminster Stairs at seven o'clock. As it turned out, it was just fast enough.

WHITEHALL—SW1 In *The Naval Treaty*, Percy Phelps worked in the Foreign Office in Whitehall.

In *The Greek Interpreter*, we learn that Holmes's older brother, Mycroft, worked in the government offices in Whitehall.

In *The Empty House,* Holmes communicated to the Foreign Office in Whitehall, details of his visit to the Khalifa of Khartoum.

BRITRAIL STATIONS

BECKENHAM was the location of the house where Mr. Melas, *The Greek Interpreter,* was taken to interpret the questioning of poor Paul Kratides. **BritRail: Beckenham Junction**

CROSS ROAD (STREET)—CROYDON Miss Susan Cushing of Cross Street, Croydon, received *The Cardboard Box* in the post. Inside, filled with coarse salt, she was horrified to find two human ears. **BritRail: East Corydon Station**

CRYSTAL PALACE—SW19 In *The Yellow Face,* Grant Munro, the hop merchant, disturbed by the actions of his wife, didn't go into the City, but walked as far as the Crystal Palace before returning home. **BritRail: Gipsy Hill Station**

FIRBANK ROAD—SE15 In *The Disappearance of Lady Frances Carfax,* Dr. Horsom of 13 Firbank Villas, was called in to certify the death of the old woman. Henry Peters, alias Rev. Dr. Shlessinger, had obtained her body from the Brixton Workhouse Infirmary. **BritRail: Queens Road (Peckham) Station**

16 IVY LANE—HOUNSLOW The Commissionaire on duty at the Foreign Office, and his wife, lived at No. 16 Ivy Lane. At first, Percy Phelps thought that they were involved in the disappearance of *The Naval Treaty.* **Brit-Rail: Hounslow Station**

KING GEORGE V (ALBERT) DOCK—SE18 This was called Albert Dock in the time of *The Cardboard Box.* Lestrade wrote; "In accordance with the scheme which we had formed in order to test our theories…I went down to the Albert Dock." Holmes thought the use of the word 'we' was rather fine. **BritRail: North Woolwich Station**

LANSDOWNE WAY (PRIORY ROAD)—SW8 In *The Sign of Four,* Holmes, Watson, and Miss Morstan were driven from the Lyceum Theatre to see Thaddeus Sholto. At one point, they turned on Priory Road. In Sherlock's day, the west part of Lansdowne Way was called Priory Road. **BritRail: Wandsworth Road Station**

LEWISHAM—SE13 Josiah Amberley, *The Retired Colourman* lived at the Haven in Lewisham. Watson went to visit Amberley, taking the train from Blackheath. Watson's observations made Holmes suspicious. **BritRail: Hither Green Station**

NORWOOD—SE27 Jonas Oldacre, *The Norwood Builder,* lived here. He planned to fake his own murder and frame John Hector McFarlane. **BritRail: West Norwood Station**

PECKHAM—SE15 In *A Study in Scarlet,* Mrs. Sawyer answered Holmes's advertisement. She said that her daughter Sally Dennis, who lived in Peckham with her husband Tom, was the one that lost the gold ring. **BritRail: Peckham Rye Station**

WALLINGTON In *The Cardboard Box,* Susan Cushing's sister Sarah, lived at New Street, Wallington. Holmes and Watson had a pleasant meal at a decent hotel in Wallington, while they waited for a reply to their telegram. **BritRail: Wallington Station**

WOOLWICH—SE18 In The *Bruce-Partington Plans,* Arthur Cadogan West worked at the Woolwich Arsenal. He left work suddenly on Monday night, and was last seen by his fiancée as he left in the fog about 7:30 that evening. In their investigation, Holmes and Watson took the train to Woolwich. The clerk at the ticket office was able to say with confidence that he saw Cadogan West Monday night, and that he went to London Bridge on the 8:15. **BritRail: North Woolwich Station**

Sherlock Holmes Adventures

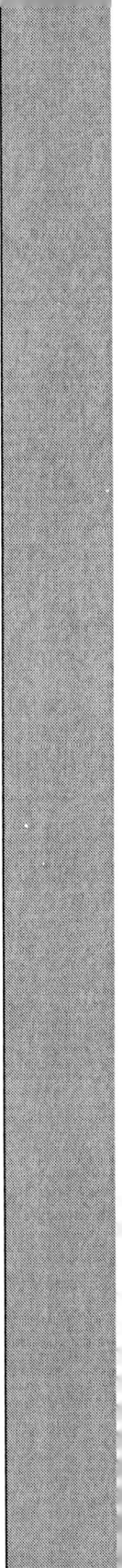

THE ADVENTURE OF ABBEY GRANGE

CHARING CROSS TRAIN STATION—Strand WC2 One early winter morning in 1897, Holmes and Watson left for Abbey Grange. They were responding to a letter from Inspector Stanley Hopkins. It wasn't until they had consumed some hot tea in Charing Cross Station, and taken their places on the Kentish train, that they were sufficiently thawed to talk about their journey. **Underground Station: Charing Cross**

CHARING CROSS—WC2 After returning from Kent, Holmes sent Inspector Hopkins a telegram from the Charing Cross telegraph office. Holmes advised him to drag the Abbey Grange pond. When Hopkins found the silver at the bottom of the pond, he thought Holmes was a wizard. **Underground Station: Charing Cross**

COCKSPUR STREET—SW1 The shipping office of the Adelaide-Southampton Line was at the end of Pall Mall, at Cockspur Street. Here Holmes learned of Captain Jack Crocker, and surmised his role in the death of Sir Eustace Brakenstall. **Underground Station: Charing Cross**

THE ADVENTURE OF THE BERYL CORONET

BAKER STREET (METROPOLITAN) UNDERGROUND STATION—W1 Watson noticed a gentleman walking towards 221B Baker Street from the direction of the Metropolitan Station. It was Alexander Holder. The Baker Street Underground Station is on the Metropolitan Line, and Watson referred to it as the "Metropolitan" Station. **Underground Station: Baker Street**

THREADNEEDLE STREET—EC2 Holder and Stevenson, the second largest private banking firm in the City, was located in Threadneedle Street. **Underground Station: Bank**

STREATHAM—SW16 Alexander Holder, a partner in Holder and Stevenson, took the precious security to his house in Streatham for safe-keeping. **Underground Station: Tooting Bec**

THE ADVENTURE OF BLACK PETER

RATCLIFF STREET AND THE HIGHWAY (RATCLIFF HIGHWAY)— E14 Holmes asked Watson to send a telegram for him. It read, "SUMNER, SHIPPING AGENT, RATCLIFF HIGHWAY. SEND THREE MEN ON, TO ARRIVE TEN TOMORROW MORNING.—BASIL." Holmes said that Basil was his name in those parts. **Underground Station: Limehouse**

THE ADVENTURE OF THE BLANCHED SOLDIER

THROGMORTON STREET—EC2 James M. Dodd was a stock-broker in Throgmorton Street. **Underground Station: Bank**

EUSTON TRAIN STATION—NW1 Holmes and James M. Dodd were joined at Euston Station by Sir James Saunders. From there, the three of them left on their trip to Tuxbury Old Park. **Underground Station: Euston**

THE ADVENTURE OF THE BLUE CARBUNCLE

KILBURN HIGH ROAD—NW6 James Ryder, Head Attendant at the Hotel Cosmopolitan, heard from his crooked friend, Maudsley, how thieves could dispose of stolen property. Maudsley lived at Kilburn. **Underground Station: Kilburn**

PENTONVILLE—N1 The Pentonville Prison was built in 1842. James Ryder's friend, Maudsley, served time in Pentonville. **Underground Station: Angel**

BRIXTON ROAD—SW9 Mrs. Oakshott lived at No. 117 Brixton Road. She sold her "city" geese to Mr. Breckinridge of Covent Garden, not knowing that James Ryder, her brother, had stuffed the jewel into the gullet of one of them. **Underground Station: Brixton**

COVENT GARDEN—WC2 Breckinridge had a stand in Covent Garden, where he sold geese. The goose he sold Windigate, proprietor of the Alpha Inn, contained the fabulous jewel. **Underground Station: Covent Garden**

GOODGE STREET and TOTTENHAM COURT ROAD—W1 This was the corner where Henry Baker lost the goose and his hat. He did not know that the Countess of Morcar's jewel was in the goose. After the fracas, Peterson, the commissionaire, ended up with both the hat and the goose. **Underground Station: Goodge Street**

WIGMORE STREET—W1 Holmes and Watson walked along Wigmore Street on their way from Baker Street to The Alpha Inn. "Our footfalls rang out crisply and loudly as we swung through the doctors' quarter, Wimpole Street, Harley Street, and so through Wigmore Street into Oxford Street. In a quarter of an hour we were in Bloomsbury at the Alpha Inn, which is a small public house at the corner of one of the streets which runs down into Holborn." **Underground Station: Oxford Circus**

HARLEY STREET—W1 Holmes and Watson passed Harley Street on their way from Baker Street to the Alpha Inn. **Underground Station: Regent's Park**

MUSEUM TAVERN (ALPHA INN), 49 Great Russell Street—WC1 This old tavern is the most likely candidate for being the Alpha Inn. Some of the regulars, including Henry Baker, instituted a goose club, which started the whole affair. **Underground Station: Tottenham Court Road**

ENDELL STREET—WC2 Holmes and Watson walked to Covent Garden from the Alpha Inn. "We passed across Holborn, down Endell Street, and so through a zigzag of slums to Covent Garden Market." **Underground Station: Covent Garden**

THE BOSCOMBE VALLEY MYSTERY

PADDINGTON STATION—W2 Watson and his wife were having breakfast, one morning, when he received a telegram from Holmes. It read: "HAVE YOU A COUPLE OF DAYS TO SPARE?…LEAVE PADDINGTON BY THE 11:15." When Watson arrived at the station, "Holmes was pacing up and down the platform, his tall gaunt figure made even gaunter and taller by his long grey traveling-cloak and the close-fitting cloth cap." **Underground Station: Paddington**

THE ADVENTURE OF THE BRUCE-PARTINGTON PLANS

WOOLWICH—SE18 Arthur Cadogan West worked at the Woolwich Arsenal. He left work suddenly, and was last seen by his fiancée when he left in the fog about 7:30 Monday evening. The clerk at the Woolwich railroad ticket office was able to say with confidence that he saw Cadogan West Monday night, when he left for London Bridge on the 8:15. **BritRail Station: North Woolwich**

ALDGATE UNDERGROUND STATION—EC3 The body of Arthur Cadogan West was found near the underground tracks, just outside Aldgate Station. They thought he had been thrown from the train, but there was no ticket in his pockets. **Underground Station: Aldgate**

ADMIRALTY, Whitehall—SW1 With the death of Arthur Cadogan West, and the missing Bruce-Partington Plans, the Admiralty was buzzing like an overturned beehive. Holmes's brother, Mycroft, had never seen the Prime Minister so upset. **Underground Station: Charing Cross**

BERKELEY (BARCLAY) SQUARE—W1 Admiral Sinclair lived on Barclay Square. Watson spelled it B-a-r-c-l-a-y, the way it is pronounced. **Underground Station: Green Park**

LONDON BRIDGE—EC4 Holmes sent his brother a telegram from London Bridge. It read: "SEE SOME LIGHT IN THE DARKNESS, BUT IT MAY POSSIBLY FLICKER OUT. MEANWHILE, PLEASE SEND…A COMPLETE LIST OF ALL FOREIGN SPIES (IN ENGLAND)." **Underground Station: Monument**

NOTTING HILL—W11 Mycroft sent Holmes a list of the biggest international spies in London, including: "Louis La Rothière of Campden Mansions, Notting Hill." **Underground Station: Notting Hill**

GREAT GEORGE STREET—SW1 Mycroft sent Holmes a list of the biggest international spies in London, including: Adolph Meyer, who had lodgings at No. 13 Great George Street. It was across Parliament Square from Westminster Bridge, near the Houses of Parliament. **Underground Station: Westminster**

CORNWALL (CAULFIELD) GARDENS—SW7 Mycroft sent Holmes a list of the biggest international spies in London, including: Hugo Oberstein, who lived in Caulfield Gardens. His townhouse backed up to the aboveground section of the Circle Line, which allowed Cadogan West's body to be placed on the roof of the train. **Underground Station: Gloucester Road**

GLOUCESTER ROAD UNDERGROUND STATION—SW7 The Circle Line Underground was clear of tunnels near the Gloucester Road Station. Herr Oberstein's windows at Caulfield Gardens overlooked the track. This gave Holmes the clue he was looking for. **Underground Station: Gloucester Road**

GLOUCESTER ROAD—SW7 Holmes asked Watson to meet him at Goldini's Restaurant in Gloucester Road. He told him to bring a revolver and burglar tools. Holmes must have liked Italian food. In another adventure, he mentions Marcini's. **Underground Station: Gloucester Road**

FLEET STREET—EC4 Holmes and Watson went to the Fleet Street district to place a newspaper advertisement. It read: "TO-NIGHT. SAME HOUR. SAME PLACE. TWO TAPS. MOST VITALLY IMPORTANT. YOUR SAFETY AT STAKE. PIERROT." **Underground Station: Holborn Viaduct**

CHARING CROSS HOTEL—Strand WC2 This famous old hotel is located at the heart of Sherlock's London. A message from Colonel Walter to Hugo Oberstein (in reality dictated by Holmes) named the Charing Cross Hotel as their meeting place. **Underground Station: Charing Cross**

THE ADVENTURE OF THE CARDBOARD BOX

CROSS ROAD—CROYDON Miss Susan Cushing, of Cross Street, Croydon, received a cardboard box in the post. Inside, filled with coarse salt, she was horrified to find two human ears. **BritRail Station: East Croydon**

KING GEORGE V (ALBERT) DOCK—SE18 This was called Albert Dock in Victorian Times. Lestrade wrote: "In accordance with the scheme which we had formed in order to test our theories…I went down to the Albert Dock." Holmes thought the use of the word 'we' was rather fine. **BritRail Station: North Woolwich**

WALLINGTON Susan Cushing's sister, Sarah, lived in Wallington. While they waited for a reply to their telegram, Holmes and Watson had a pleasant little meal at a decent hotel there. **BritRail Station: Wallington**

TOTTENHAM COURT ROAD—WC1 While Holmes and Watson were having their lunch in Wallington, Holmes told how he bought his Stradivarius from a Jew broker in Tottenham Court Road for fifty-five shillings. It was worth at least five hundred guineas. **Underground Station: Tottenham Court Road**

A CASE OF IDENTITY

KING'S CROSS—WC1 Mary Sutherland's stepfather, in an attempt to keep her money at home, disguised himself as Hosmer Angel. Poor Mary planned to marry Angel at St. Saviour's Church, near King's Cross. **Underground Station: King's Cross/St. Pancras**

MIDLAND GRAND (ST. PANCRAS) HOTEL—2 St. Chad Street WC1 Mary Sutherland had planned her wedding breakfast at the St Pancras Hotel. One of the grand railroad hotels built in the mid-nineteenth century, the St. Pancras is now called the Midland Grand Hotel. **Underground Station: King's Cross/St. Pancras**

CAMBERWELL—SE5 Mary Sutherland lived in Camberwell. She didn't know Mr. Angel's address. **Underground Station: Brixton**

FENCHURCH STREET—EC3 Mary Sutherland's stepfather, James Windibank, worked for Westhouse and Marbank, the great claret importers of Fenchurch Street. **Underground Station: Aldgate**

LEADENHALL STREET—EC3 Hosmer Angel, who in reality was Mary Sutherland's stepfather in disguise, was supposedly a cashier in an office in Leadenhall Street. Mary didn't know which office. **Underground Station: Aldgate**

THE ADVENTURE OF CHARLES AUGUSTUS MILVERTON

HAMPSTEAD—NW3 Charles Augustus Milverton, who Holmes called "the worst man in London," lived in Appledore Towers, Hampstead. One splendid night, Holmes and Watson went to Hampstead to burgle Milverton's house. **Underground Station: Hampstead**

CHURCH ROW—NW3 On their way to burgle Milverton's house, Holmes and Watson took a cab as far as Church Row. **Underground Station: Hampstead**

REGENT'S PARK ZOO—NW1 Holmes told Watson that Milverton reminded him of the serpents in the Regent's Park Zoo. "And yet I can't get out of doing business with him." **Underground Station: Camden Town**

OXFORD (REGENT) CIRCUS—W1 After the murder of Milverton, Holmes and Watson hurried down Oxford Street to a shop near Regent Circus. There in the window they saw a picture of a regal and stately lady in court dress. Holmes put his finger to his lips, indicating that they must keep the secret. **Underground Station: Oxford Circus**

THE ADVENTURE OF THE CREEPING MAN

COMMERCIAL STREET (ROAD)—E1 Holmes stopped at a post office and sent off a telegram. Mercer's reply reached him that evening. It read: "HAVE VISITED THE COMMERCIAL ROAD AND SEEN DORAK. SUAVE PERSON, BOHEMIAN, ELDERLY. KEEPS LARGE GENERAL STORE." **Underground Station: Aldgate East**

THE ADVENTURE OF THE DANCING MEN

RUSSELL SQUARE—WC1 Hilton Cubitt came to London for the Jubilee. He stayed in a boardinghouse in Russell Square. There he met the American, Elsie Parker. After their marriage, Elsie started receiving the dancing men messages. **Underground Station: Russell Square**

LIVERPOOL STATION—EC2 Hilton Cubitt wrote Holmes, asking for an appointment. Holmes asked Watson to remain at Baker Street, because Cubitt might arrive at any moment. **Underground Station: Liverpool**

THE ADVENTURE OF THE DEVIL'S FOOT

HARLEY STREET—W1 Harley Street is the home of well-placed West End physicians. Doctor Moore Agar, of #6 Harley Street, advised Holmes to take a country rest, or suffer a complete breakdown. Holmes and Watson went to Cornwall and found the Devil's Foot. **Underground Station: Regent's Park**

THE ADVENTURE OF THE DYING DETECTIVE

LADBROKE GROVE (LOWER BURKE STREET)—W11 Although the name was modified, Ladbroke Grove fits the location of Lower Burke Street, where Mr. Culverton Smith rented a house "in the vague borderland between Notting Hill and Kensington." Smith was a well-known resident of Sumatra and an expert on oriental diseases. **Underground Station: Notting Hill Gate**

ROTHERHITHE—SE18 In Victorian times, this dockside area, across the Thames from Wapping, was a very rough place. Holmes supposedly picked up a coolie disease in Rotherhithe, and returned to Baker Street to die. **Underground Station: Rotherhithe**

SIMPSON'S IN THE STRAND—100 Strand WC2 Simpson's, arguable the best-known English restaurant in London, hasn't changed much since the 1890's. After his three day fast, Holmes told Watson, "Something nutritious at Simpson's would not be out of place." **Underground Station: Temple**

THE ADVENTURE OF THE EMPTY HOUSE

PARK LANE—W1 Ronald Adair, second son of the Earl of Maynooth, lived at No. 427 Park Lane (old numbering). He played cards with, and was later murdered by, Colonel Sebastian Moran. Holmes thought that Adair had caught Moran cheating. Later, after strolling from Hyde Park, Watson walked by the site of the murder. He bumped into an elderly bibliophile carrying several books. He didn't know it at the time, but it was Holmes in disguise. **Underground Station: Marble Arch**

CHURCH STREET—W8. Before revealing his true identity, the old bibliophile told Watson that they were neighbors in Kensington. He said he had a little bookstore at the corner of Church Street. **Underground Station: High Street Kensington**

CONDUIT STREET—W1 We learn from Holmes's index of biographies, that Colonel Sebastian Moran was the second most dangerous man in London. He lodged in Conduit Street. **Underground Station: Oxford Circus**

CAVENDISH SQUARE—W1 Holmes stopped the cab at Cavendish Square, as he did at every subsequent street corner, to assure that he and Watson were not being followed. **Underground Station: Oxford Circus**

MANCHESTER STREET—W1 Holmes and Watson drove on Manchester Street, on their way to Camden House. **Underground Station: Baker Street**

BLANDFORD STREET—W1 Holmes and Watson turned left from Manchester Street to Blandford Street on their way to Camden House. **Underground Station: Baker Street**

32 or 34 BAKER STREET (CAMDEN HOUSE)—W1 Holmes and Watson went to the empty Camden House, just across Baker Street from 221B. There they lay in wait for Colonel Sebastian Moran. Based on the route described, and other clues, the most likely location of Camden House is either today's #32 or #34 Baker Street. Since Holmes and Watson lived opposite, the most likely location of 221B was the house formerly at today's #31 Baker Street. **Underground Station: Baker Street**

CHARING CROSS RAILWAY STATION, STRAND—WC2 In this adventure, we learn that Holmes had his canine tooth knocked out by Mathews, in the Charing Cross waiting room, **Underground Station: Charing Cross**

FOREIGN OFFICE, KING CHARLES STREET—SW1 In this adventure, we learn that Holmes had communicated to the Foreign Office, details of his visit to the Khalifa of Khartoum. **Underground Station: Westminster**

SCOTLAND YARD (NEW), Derby Gate—SW1 "New" Scotland Yard opened in 1891, near Westminster Bridge. It figured prominently in many of Sherlock's cases.

In their Black Museum, Scotland Yard kept the air gun that Colonel Moran used when he tried to kill Holmes. **Underground Station: Westminster**

THE ADVENTURE OF THE ENGINEER'S THUMB

GREENWICH—SE10 Victor Hatherley had been apprenticed to Venner & Matheson, the well-known engineering firm in Greenwich. After he went into business for himself, he got into a situation that resulted in the loss of his thumb. **Underground Station: Greenwich**

PADDINGTON TRAIN STATION—W2 In the Summer of 1889, Victor Hatherley departed from Paddington Train Station to meet Colonel Lysander Stark near Reading. This misadventure resulted in the loss of Hatherley's thumb. Later, the maid woke Watson to announce that two men had arrived from Paddington Station. One of them needed medical attention. **Underground Station: Paddington**

VICTORIA STREET—SW1 Victor Hatherley lived in a third floor walk-up at 16A Victoria Street. **Underground Station: Victoria**

THE FINAL PROBLEM

MARYLEBONE LANE—W1 Holmes passed the corner which leads from Bentinck to the Welbeck Street crossing. He was almost hit by a two-horse van that "dashed round by Marylebone Lane, and was gone in an instant." **Underground Station: Bond Street**

WELBECK and BENTINCK STREETS—W1 Holmes was nearly killed at this intersection. He thought that Professor Moriarty might be behind the "accident." **Underground: Bond Street**

VERE STREET—W1 A brick fell from a Vere Street building, shattering at Holmes's feet. This was just after the near "accident" at Bentinck and Welbeck streets. This convinced Holmes that Professor Moriarty was trying to kill him. **Underground Station: Bond Street**

MORTIMER STREET—W1 At the time of this adventure, Watson was married and in private practice. He lived in a house that backed up to Mortimer Street. Holmes visited him there, as they made plans to elude Professor Moriarty. In fear of an air gun attack, Holmes clambered over the back wall into Mortimer Street. **Underground Station: Oxford Street**

440 STRAND—WC2 This was the site of the Lowther Arcade. Holmes instructed Watson to exit the hansom at the Strand front entrance, dash through the Arcade to the Adelaide Street back entrance. **Underground Station: Charing Cross**

ADELAIDE STREET—WC2 The former Lowther Arcade had its back entrance on Adelaide Street. Holmes instructed Watson to enter the waiting brougham on Adelaide Street. Holmes's brother, Mycroft, was the driver. **Underground Station: Charing Cross**

VICTORIA STATION—SW1 Watson followed Holmes's instructions to the letter. After his dash through the Lowther Arcade, he arrived at Victoria Station just in time to catch the Continental express. Moriarty was close behind. **Underground Station: Victoria**

GROSVENOR HOTEL—SW1 Holmes and Watson reached the little Alpine village of Meiringen. There, they stayed at the Englischer Hof, which was kept by Peter Steiler the elder. He spoke excellent English, having served more than three years as waiter, at the Grosvenor Hotel in London. **Underground Station: Victoria**

THE FIVE ORANGE PIPS

WATERLOO BRIDGE—SE1 After receiving a threat from the Klu Klux Klan, John Openshaw consulted Holmes. Later, on his way to Waterloo Station, Openshaw was thrown from the Embankment into the Thames near Waterloo Bridge. **Underground Station: Embankment**

VICTORIA EMBANKMENT—WC2 Holmes, wonders how members of the Klan decoyed John Openshaw from Waterloo Bridge to the Embankment, where he was thrown into the Thames. **Underground Station: Embankment**

LLOYD'S OF LONDON, Fenchurch Street—EC3 Holmes spent the day at Lloyd's, going over their files to trace the ship, "Lone Star." **Underground Station: Aldgate**

THE ADVENTURE OF THE GOLDEN PINCE-NEZ

CHARING CROSS RAILWAY STATION, Strand—WC2 Stanley Hopkins, the young detective, arrived at Baker Street late one night. He had just returned to Charing Cross Station, on the last train. He asked Holmes and Watson to accompany him back to Yoxley Old Place the next morning. **Underground Station: Charing Cross**

THE GREEK INTERPRETER

WHITEHALL—SW1 In this adventure, we learn that Holmes's older brother, Mycroft, worked at the government offices in Whitehall. **Underground Station: Westminster**

PALL MALL—SW1 Mycroft's chambers were in Pall Mall, with his Diogenes Club just opposite. Melas, the interpreter, had lodgings on the floor above Mycroft. **Underground Station: Charring Cross**

NORTHUMBERLAND AVENUE—SW1 Between where Great Scotland Yard, and Whitehall Place, run into Northumberland Avenue, there is a building that once was the Hotel Metropole. Mr. Melas acted as a guide to the wealthy Orientals who stayed at the "grand" Northumberland Avenue hotels. **Underground Station: Charing Cross**

VICTORIA STATION—SW1 After his strange experience, Mr. Melas was just able to return to Victoria Station on the last train from Clapham Junction. He related the story to Mycroft Holmes, who knew that Sherlock would be interested. **Underground Station: Victoria**

OXFORD STREET—W1 Holmes and Watson walked on Oxford Street toward Regent Circus. They were on their way to the Diogenes Club in Pall Mall, to meet Holmes's older brother, Mycroft. They must have turned south before they reached the Circus, because they reached Pall Mall from the St. James's Street end. **Underground Station: Oxford Circus**

ST. JAMES'S STREET—SW1 On their way to Mycroft's club in Pall Mall, Holmes and Watson walked down St. James's Street. **Underground Station: Green Park**

CHARING CROSS—WC2 A four-wheeled carriage collected Mr. Melas at his Pall Mall lodgings. As they started off through Charing Cross, he was told they were going to Kensington. **Underground Station: Charing Cross**

SHAFTESBURY AVENUE—W1. The carriage with Mr. Melas continued up Shaftesbury Avenue towards Oxford Street. **Underground Station: Piccadilly Circus**

OXFORD STREET—W1. When the carriage reached Oxford Street, Mr. Melas commented that this was a roundabout way to Kensington. At that point, the windows were covered. **Underground Bond Street**

BECKENHAM was the real location of the house, where Mr. Melas was taken. There, he was ordered to interpret the questioning of Paul Kratides. **BritRail Station: Beckenham Junction**

WANDSWORTH COMMON—SW11 Mr. Melas was forced to interpret poor Paul Kratides late into the night. Afterwards, Melas was let out in Wandsworth Common. **Underground Station: Clapham South**

CLAPHAM JUNCTION—SW11 After walking across Wandsworth Common to Clapham Junction, Mr. Melas was just in time to catch the last train to Victoria Station. **Underground Station: Clapham North**

BRIXTON ROAD—SW9 J. Davenport, from Lower Brixton, answered Mycroft Holmes's advertisement in the Daily News. **Underground Station: Brixton**

LONDON BRIDGE STATION—EC4 It took an hour in Scotland Yard before Inspector Gregson could get a warrant to enter the house in Beckenham, and then it was a 40-minute train ride from London Bridge Station to Beckenham Junction. **Underground Station: London Bridge**

HIS LAST BOW

OLYMPIA—W14 Von Bork was the ideal German agent for Great Britain. Being a sportsman, he competed with the British aristocracy in sailing, hunting and polo. He even matched them by taking a prize in The Horse of the Year competition at Olympia. **Underground Station: Olympia**

ADMIRALTY—Whitehall, SW1 Baron Von Herling complained that The Admiralty had received an alarm on the Naval Signals he had been accumulating, and had changed every code. **Underground Station: Charing Cross**

CARLTON HOUSE TERRACE (CARLTON TERRACE)—SW1 On the Duke of York's Steps, near the Duke's Column, there are two small doors. The easternmost was near the German Embassy. Von Bork was told: "When you get the signal book through the little door…you can put a finis to your record in England." **Underground Station: Charing Cross**

CLARIDGE'S (HOTEL)—**Brook Street, W1** After capturing Von Bork, Holmes needed to shave off his goatee before reappearing as himself at Claridge's. **Underground Station: Bond Street**

THE HOUND OF THE BASKERVILLES

CHARING CROSS—**WC2** In *The Hound of the Baskervilles*, friends, at the old Charing Cross Hospital, gave Dr. Mortimer an engraved walking stick. Later, he came to London to meet Sir Henry Baskerville, newly arrived from Canada. Sir Henry received a letter at the Northumberland Hotel with the postmark of the Charing Cross Post Office. Holmes wondered how the sender knew that Sir Henry was staying at the Northumberland. **Underground Station: Charing Cross**

WILLIAM IV AND AGAR STREETS—**WC2** The old Charing Cross Hospital was located in the triangular site where William IV and Agar Streets meet the Strand. **Underground Station: Charing Cross**

WATERLOO RAIL STATION—**SE1** Sir Henry Baskerville arrived in London at the Waterloo Rail Station. Dr. Mortimer came to London to meet him. **Underground Station: Waterloo**

ROYAL COLLEGE OF SURGEONS, **35/43 Lincoln's Inn Fields—WC2** Dr. Mortimer spent the afternoon at the Museum of the College of Surgeons, without Sir Henry. **Underground Station: Holborn**

CRAVEN STREET—**WC2** Stapleton brought his wife to London and lodged at the Mexborough Private Hotel in Craven Street. He kept her imprisoned in the room while he followed Dr. Mortimer to Baker Street, and later to the Northumberland Hotel. **Underground Station: Embankment**

GREAT SCOTLAND YARD—**WC2,** On the west side of Northumberland Avenue, from Great Scotland Yard south to Whitehall Place, was the site of The Metropole, the most likely candidate for being The Northumberland Hotel. In 1888, Sir Henry Baskerville stayed there when he received the warning message: "AS YOU VALUE YOUR LIFE...KEEP AWAY FROM THE MOOR." While at the hotel, he also lost a new brown boot, and then, when it reappeared, an old black boot was taken. This gave Sherlock a clue. **Underground Station: Embankment**

SHERLOCK HOLMES PUB, 10 Northumberland Street—WC2 In 1883, this building changed its name from The Northumberland Hotel, to The Northumberland Arms. The new name more correctly reflected its character as a modest hostelry. As such, it could not have been the "Northumberland Hotel", at which the wealthy Sir Henry Baskerville stayed in 1888. Today, this pub is a Mecca for fans of Sherlock Holmes. In addition to traditional pub grub and drinks, they have an excellent upstairs restaurant, complete with a replica of the 221B Baker Street sitting room. **Underground Station: Embankment**

THE STRAND—WC2 Sir Henry, who had just arrived from Canada, bought a new pair of brown boots in the Strand. He paid six dollars for them, and one was stolen before he even had them on his feet. **Underground Station: Charing Cross**

STANFORDS (STAMFORD'S), 12-14 Long Acre—WC2 This famous map shop was founded in 1852. Holmes sent to Stamford's for a large-scale Ordnance map of that part of Devonshire that included Baskerville Hall. **Underground Station: Covent Garden**

OXFORD STREET—W1. In this adventure, it was mentioned that both Holmes and Watson used Bradley's, in Oxford Street, as their tobacconist. They supplied Holmes with his strong shag, and Watson with his cigarettes. Dr. Mortimer and Baskerville also walked down Oxford Street to Regent Street, on their way to the Northumberland Hotel. Holmes and Watson trailed behind, trying to see who was following them. **Underground Station: Bond Street**

REGENT STREET—W1 Holmes and Watson followed Sir Henry along Regent Street, and noticed someone following in a hansom cab. After the hansom cab sped away, Holmes enlisted the help of young Cartwright, who worked in the district messenger service office in Regent Street. Holmes told him to go to each of the twenty-three hotels in the Charing Cross area, and see if he could find a clue. **Underground Station: Piccadilly Circus**

BOND STREET—W1 While waiting for young Cartwright's report, Holmes and Watson spent the afternoon in the Bond Street picture galleries. Holmes was absorbed in the pictures of the modern Belgian masters. **Underground Station: Bond Street**

SOUTHWARK—SE1 Holmes located the driver of the hansom cab that followed Sir Henry and Dr. Mortimer. His name was John Clayton, and he lived in the Borough of Southwark. Holmes made a note of it. **Underground Station: Waterloo**

WATERLOO TRAIN STATION—SE1 John Clayton worked out of Shipley's Yard, near Waterloo Train Station. **Underground Station: Waterloo**

TRAFALGAR SQUARE—WC2 Clayton said he picked up his fare at Trafalgar Square, and that his passenger said he was Sherlock Holmes. This alerted Holmes as to the character of his adversary. **Underground Station: Charing Cross**

PADDINGTON TRAIN STATION—W2 Watson, Dr. Mortimer, and Sir Henry left London from Paddington station, on their way to Devon and Baskerville Hall. **Underground Station: Paddington**

BRITISH MUSEUM, GREAT RUSSELL STREET—WC1 Holmes discovered that the Vandeleurs had established a school in the east of Yorkshire. When it failed, they changed their names to Stapleton and moved to the South of England. The British Museum considered Stapleton a recognized authority in entomology. **Underground Station: Tottenham Court Road**

FULHAM ROAD—SW6 Stapleton bought the hound from Ross & Mangles, dog dealers in Fulham Road. **Underground Station: Fulham Broadway**

ROYAL OPERA HOUSE—Covent Garden, WC2 Completed in 1858, this is London's leading opera house. After the successful conclusion of the adventure, Holmes reserved a box at the Royal Opera House for "Les Huguenots." **Underground Station: Covent Garden**

THE ADVENTURE OF THE ILLUSTRIOUS CLIENT

CARLTON CLUB—SW1 Formed in 1832, the Carlton Club moved four years later to Pall Mall, near the Duke of York's Column. Sir James Damery wrote Holmes from the Carlton. He wanted to consult Holmes on Violet de Merville's infatuation with Baron Gruner. Today, the Carlton Club is located at 69 St. James's Street, SW1. **Underground Station: Charing Cross**

HURLINGHAM PARK—SW6 Holmes accepted the commission from Sir James, on behalf of an illustrious client. Watson mused about what he knew about Baron Gruner, "He has expensive tastes. He is a horse fancier. For a short time he played polo at Hurlingham." **Underground Station: Putney Bridge**

BERKELEY SQUARE—W1 General de Merville, of Khyber fame, and his daughter Violet, lived at 104 Berkeley Square. It was, "one of those…London castles which would make a church seem frivolous." **Underground Station: Green Park**

SIMPSON'S IN THE STRAND—100 Strand, WC2 Simpson's restaurant hasn't changed much since the 1890's. When Watson joined Holmes at a table in Simpson's window, Holmes said, "Johnson is on the prowl." Holmes had turned to Shinwell Johnson to gain access to his underworld contacts. **Underground Station: Temple**

ST. JAMES'S SQUARE—SW1 The London Library is still located in St. James's Square. It was founded in 1841 by Thomas Carlyle, as an alternative to the library at the British Museum. Watson needed twenty-four hours of intensive study to pose as an expert on Chinese pottery. His friend Lomax, the Sub Librarian, helped him find the books he needed. **Underground Station: Piccadilly Circus**

HALF MOON STREET—W1 Watson, under his alias, Dr. Hill Barton, supposedly lived at No. 369 Half Moon Street. As Barton, he went to see Baron Gruner about the blue Ming saucer. **Underground Station: Green Park**

CHRISTIE'S AUCTION HOUSE, 8 King Street—SW1 This famous firm was founded in 1766. If pressed for a price, Watson was to suggest that Christie's or Sotheby's set the value of the blue Ming saucer. **Underground Station: Green Park**

SOTHEBY'S AUCTION HOUSE, New Bond Street—W1 Watson, posing as Dr. Hill Barton, took the Ming saucer to Baron Gruner's. If pressed for a price, Watson was to suggest that Christie's or Sotheby's set the value. **Underground Station: Bond Street**

CAFÉ ROYAL—68 Regent Street, W1 Two men attacked Holmes near the Café Royal. They were armed with sticks. **Underground Station: Piccadilly Circus**

GLASSHOUSE STREET—W1 Holmes escaped by running through the Café Royal, into Glasshouse Street. **Underground Station: Piccadilly Circus**

NORTHUMBERLAND AVENUE—SW1 Watson was walking on Northumberland between the Grand Hotel and Charing Cross Station, when a one-legged newsvendor displayed the headline: "MURDEROUS ATTACK UPON SHERLOCK HOLMES." Watson felt a pang of horror. **Underground Station: Charing Cross**

BETWEEN GREAT SCOTLAND YARD AND WHITEHALL PLACE ON NORTHUMBERLAND AVENUE—SW1 The Metropole Hotel was located on the west side of Northumberland Avenue, between Great Scotland Yard and Whitehall Place. This is the most likely candidate for being "the…select London hotel," where Francis Hay Moulton was a guest. "Eight shillings for a bed, and eightpence for a glass of sherry," gave Holmes a clue. "There are not many (hotels) in London which charge at that rate." **Underground Station: Embankment**

WILLIAM IV AND AGAR STREETS—WC2 The old Charing Cross Hospital was located in the triangular site, where William IV and Agar Streets meet the Strand. Holmes was brought here after the attack. **Underground Station: Charing Cross**

CRAVEN STREET—WC2 Watson mentioned that he and Holmes had a weakness for the Turkish bath. Theirs was the Charing Cross Turkish Bath. It was located in the wedged shaped building, where Craven Street joins Northumberland Avenue. The women's entrance was through Craven Passage, which in Sherlock's time was called Northumberland Passage. **Underground Station: Embankment**

QUEEN ANNE STREET—W1 We also learn that Watson, who Sherlock called his "Boswell", has his surgery at No. 9 Queen Anne Street. Conan Doyle placed it here as a tribute to the original Boswell, James, who lived in Queen Anne Street when he wrote the *Life of Samuel Johnson.* **Underground Station: Bond Street**

THE DISAPPEARANCE OF LADY FRANCES CARFAX

CAMBERWELL—SE5 Lady Frances Carfax wrote her old governess, Miss Dobney, every second week. Miss Dobney lived in Camberwell. When Lady Frances stopped this regular custom, it alerted Holmes that something was amiss. **Underground Station: Brixton**

LANGHAM HOTEL—Portland Place, W1 This very exclusive Victorian hotel has been restored to its former glory. During Holmes's time, the fact that you were a guest at the Langham automatically marked you as a gentleman. The Hon. Philip Green, the son of a famous admiral of the same name, stayed at the Langham. **Underground Station: Oxford Circus**

FIRBANK ROAD—SE15 Dr. Horsom, of 13 Firbank Villas, was called in to certify the death of the old woman that Henry Peters, alias The Rev. Dr. Shlessinger, had obtained from the Brixton Workhouse Infirmary. **BritRail Station: Queens Road (Peckham)**

KENNINGTON ROAD—SE11 Stimson and Co., the undertaker in Kennington Road, made the "out of the ordinary" casket for the evil Dr. Shlessinger and his wife. The casket was deep enough for two bodies. **Underground: Kennington**

BRIXTON ROAD—SW9 Holmes and Watson used a route along Brixton Road to Dr. Shlessinger house in Poultney Square. **Underground Station: Brixton**

OXFORD STREET—W1 In the 1890's, Oxford Street was as busy as it is today. In this adventure, we discover that Watson bought his boots at Latimer's in Oxford Street. **Underground Station: Bond Street**

THE MAN WITH THE TWISTED LIP

THREADNEEDLE STREET—EC2 Neville St. Clair, as Hugh Boone, spent his days in Threadneedle Street, selling wax vestas. **Underground Station: Bank**

CANNON STREET TRAIN STATION—EC4 St. Clair returned home to Kent every evening from the Cannon Street Station. He never told his wife how he earned his money. **Underground Station: Cannon Street**

UPPER THAMES STREET (UPPER SWANDAM LANE)—EC4. Having found herself in a very bad part of town, Mrs. St. Clair walked down Upper Swandam Lane trying to find a cab. To her surprise, she saw her husband in a second-floor window. When she returned with several constables to search the building, her husband had disappeared. Holmes knew the building was an opium den. He said, "There is a trapdoor at the back of the building…which could tell some strange tales." **Underground Station: Mansion House**

PAUL'S WALK—EC4 This was the location of Paul's Wharf. Holmes said the opium den on Upper Swandam Lane had a trapdoor in the rear, near Paul's Wharf. **Underground Station: Mansion House**

WATERLOO BRIDGE ROAD—SE1 Holmes and Watson returned to London from Neville St. Clair's home in Kent. They traveled down Waterloo Bridge Road on their way to the Bow Street Police Court. **Underground Station: Waterloo**

WELLINGTON and BOW STREETS—WC2 From Waterloo Bridge Road, Holmes and Watson traveled up Wellington Street, on their way to Bow Street. There, at the old Police Court, they solved the mystery. **Underground Station: Covent Garden**

BOW STREET POLICE COURT—WC2 Inspector Bradstreet was on duty at Bow Street when Holmes and Watson arrived. They unmasked Hugh Boone, who was in fact, Neville St. Clair, in disguise.

Founded in 1740, this famous police court was the home of the pre-Scotland Yard London policemen. They were called the Bow Street Runners and were paid by the capture, much as bounty hunters are today. **Underground Station: Covent Garden**

THE ADVENTURE OF THE MAZARIN STONE

10 DOWNING STREET—SW1 No. 10 is the traditional home of the British Heads of Government. This must have been the place from which the Prime Minister came, to consult Holmes about the missing Crown Jewel. **Underground Station: Westminster**

221B BAKER STREET—W1 In this adventure, we learn that Holmes's second floor bedroom had three doors: one leading to the sitting-room, a second exit to the hallway (where Holmes could see arriving guests), and a hidden third door that opened behind the curtains. **Underground Station: Baker Street**

LIME STREET—EC3 This ancient street in the City, was named for the sellers of limes, who once congregated there. Count Sylvius said he would have to go to Lime Street to give the stone to Van Seddar. **Underground Station: Monument**

MINORIES—EC3 Holmes followed Count Negretto Sylvius to old Straubenzee's workshop in the Minories. Straubenzee made the air gun that Holmes thought was pointed at him from a window on the other side of Baker Street. Holmes had a target dummy made, in his likeness. **Underground Station: Tower Hill**

THE ADVENTURE OF THE MISSING THREE-QUARTER

THE STRAND—WC2 In the 1890s, the Strand was the center of London's West End. Holmes received a telegram from Cyril Overton. It was sent from the Strand Post Office, and read: "PLEASE AWAIT ME. TERRIBLE MISFORTUNE. RIGHT WING THREE-QUARTER MISSING, INDISPENSABLE TO-MORROW." **Underground Station: Charing Cross**

BLACKHEATH—SE12 Overton was amazed that Holmes had never heard of Godfrey Staunton, the three-quarter who played on the Cambridge and Blackheath Rugby teams. **Underground Station: Greenwich**

KING'S CROSS TRAIN STATION—N1 Holmes and Watson left King's Cross Station on their way to Cambridge. **Underground Station: King's Cross**

THE MUSGRAVE RITUAL

MONTAGUE STREET—WC1 Holmes said that after college, when he first came to London, he had rooms in Montague Street. He wanted to be near the British Museum's Reading Room. **Underground Station: Holborn**

BRITISH MUSEUM—Great Russell Street—WC1 The Museum's world famous Reading Room contains an enormous collection of scientific works. When he first came to London, young Sherlock studied those branches of science, which would later make him so efficient. **Underground Station: Tottenham Court Road**

HOUSES OF PARLIAMENT—SW1 Reginald Musgrave visited Holmes at his room in Montague Street. Musgrave said that his father had died, and now, in addition to now having to manage the estate, he was also a Member of Parliament for his district. **Underground Station: Westminster**

THE NAVAL TREATY

WHITEHALL—SW1 After he left Cambridge, Percy Phelps went to work at the Foreign Office in Whitehall. **Underground Station: Westminster**

KING CHARLES STREET—SW1 Whoever stole the treaty, entered and left the Foreign Office through the side door in King Charles Street. **Underground Station: Westminster**

16 IVY LANE—HOUNSLOW The Commissionaire who was on duty at the Foreign Office, and his wife, lived at No. 16 Ivy Lane. At first, Percy Phelps thought that they were involved in the disappearance of the treaty. **BritRail Station: Hounslow**

DOWNING STREET—SW1 Lord Holdhurst, Percy Phelps's uncle, had chambers in Downing Street. Holmes was able to find the missing treaty, and save poor Percy's honor. **Underground Station: Westminster**

WATERLOO TRAIN STATION—SE1 Holmes and Watson caught an early train from Waterloo to Woking. They were answering a plea for help from Percy Phelps, Watson's old school chum. **Underground Station: Waterloo**

CLAPHAM JUNCTION—SW11 Joseph Harrison drove Holmes and Watson to the station. There, they caught the Portsmouth train to London. As they passed Clapham Junction, Holmes remarked, "It's a very cheering thing to come into London by any of these lines which run high and allow you to look down on houses like this." Watson thought he was joking. **Underground Station: Clapham North**

THE ADVENTURE OF THE NOBLE BACHELOR

BETWEEN GREAT SCOTLAND YARD AND WHITEHALL PLACE IN NORTHUMBERLAND AVENUE—SW1 This is the site of the old Hotel Metropole. Many Sherlockian scholars think that this was the hotel at which Francis Hay Moulton stayed, when he first came to London to search for Hatty. Today, the closest "grand" hotel is The Royal Horseguards. **Underground Station: Embankment**

LANCASTER GATE—W2 Aloysius Doran, the wealthy American, took a furnished house at Lancaster Gate. His only daughter, Hatty, was to marry Lord Robert St. Simon. It was here, during the wedding breakfast, that Hatty disappeared. **Underground Station: Lancaster Gate**

HYDE PARK—W2 Hatty Doran St. Simon was seen walking in Hyde Park with Flora Millar. Flora had been on a "very friendly footing" with Lord St. Simon, and had created a disturbance at the wedding breakfast. In a futile effort to find Hatty, Inspector Lestrade began dragging the Serpentine. **Underground Station: Marble Arch**

TRAFALGAR SQUARE FOUNTAIN—WC2 When Inspector Lestrade told Holmes that the Serpentine was being dragged, Holmes laughed and asked if he was also dragging the Trafalgar Square Fountain, "Because you have just as good a chance of finding this lady in the one as in the other." **Underground Station: Charing Cross**

ST. GEORGE'S HANOVER SQUARE—2a Mill Street, W1 St. George's was the church in which Lord Robert St. Simon, second son of the Duke of Balmoral, was to marry Miss Hatty Doran. **Underground Station: Oxford Circus**

GORDON SQUARE—WC1 Francis Hay Moulton took lodgings at No. 226 Gordon Square. He and Hatty went there after her disappearance. **Underground Station: Euston Square**

THE ADVENTURE OF THE NORWOOD BUILDER

NORWOOD—SE27 Jonas Oldacre, the builder, lived in Norwood. He planned to fake his own murder and frame John Hector McFarlane. **BritRail: West Norwood**

GRESHAM HOUSE, HOLBORN VIADUCT—EC1 John Hector McFarlane was a junior partner in Graham and McFarlane of 426 Gresham Buildings. **Underground Station: St. Paul's**

LONDON BRIDGE STATION—EC4 The unhappy John Hector McFarlane came to see Holmes. He knew that he was followed from London Bridge Station. **Underground Station: London Bridge**

BLACKHEATH—SE12 In their attempt to help John Hector McFarlane, Holmes and Watson first went in the direction of Blackheath. **Underground Station: Greenwich**

THE ADVENTURE OF THE PRIORY SCHOOL

ADMIRALTY, WHITEHALL—SW1 The Duke of Holdernesse had been Lord of the Admiralty, with offices at Whitehall. **Underground Station: Westminster**

CARLTON HOUSE TERRACE—SW1 The Duke's London residence was in Carlton House Terrace. **Underground Station: Charing Cross**

EUSTON TRAIN STATION—NW1 Holmes, Watson, and Dr. Huxtable, left from Euston Station en route to Mackleton. **Underground Station: Euston**

OXFORD STREET—W1 Holmes deposited the Duke's check in the Oxford Street branch of Holmes's bank. **Underground Station: Bond Street**

THE PROBLEM OF THOR BRIDGE

CLARIDGE'S (HOTEL)—**Brook Street, W1** J. Neil Gibson wrote Holmes from Claridge's. **Underground Station: Bond Street**

CRAIG'S COURT—SW1 Cox and King's Bank was located in this small court near Charing Cross. Watson said, "in the vaults of Cox and Co., at Charing Cross, there is a travel-worn and battered tin dispatch box with my name…painted on it." **Underground Station: Charing Cross**

THE ADVENTURE OF THE RED CIRCLE

GREAT ORMOND (ORME) STREET—WC1 The Warrens lived in a "high, thin, yellow-brick edifice" in Great Orme Street. Mrs. Warren consulted Holmes about her strange lodger, who was Emilia Lucca, although no one knew it at the time. **Underground Station: Russell Square**

TOTTENHAM COURT ROAD—WC1 Mr. Warren was a timekeeper at Morton and Waylight's in Tottenham Court Road. **Underground Station: Goodge Street**

HAMPSTEAD HEATH—NW3 Mrs. Warren didn't know what to make of the strange behavior of her lodger. Mrs. Warren reached her limit, when her husband was abducted and dropped off on Hampstead Heath. **Underground Station: Hampstead**

ROYAL OPERA HOUSE, COVENT GARDEN—WC2 Completed in 1858, this is London's leading opera house. Holmes said, "By the way, it is not eight o'clock, and a Wagner night at Covent Garden! If we hurry, we might be in time for the second act." **Underground Station: Covent Garden**

THE RED-HEADED LEAGUE

POPPINS (POPE'S) COURT—EC4 Duncan Ross, alias: William Morris, advertised for all red-headed men to apply at the offices of the League at No. 7 Pope's Court, just off Fleet Street. **Underground Station: Blackfriars**

17 KING EDWARD STREET—EC1. Jabez Wilson went to the offices of *The Red-headed League* to do his daily task and found the door locked. He was told that Duncan Ross was really solicitor William Morris, and that he had moved to new offices at 17 King Edward Street, near St. Paul's. **Underground Station: St. Paul's**

BARBICAN (ALDERSGATE) UNDERGROUND STATION—EC3 Holmes and Watson got off the underground at Aldersgate, (now called Barbican) Station, on their way to Jabez Wilson's small pawnshop. Holmes thumped the pavement with his stick, checking for tunnels. **Underground Station: Barbican**

THE STRAND—WC2 In the 1890s, the Strand was the center of London's West End. McFarlane's carriage-building depot was in the Strand, next to the Vegetarian Restaurant. **Underground Station: Charing Cross**

FARRINGDON (FARRINGTON) STREET—EC4 Holmes, Watson, Inspector Jones, and Mr. Merryweather, drove along Farrington Street on their way to the bank. There, they captured John Clay. **Underground Station: Farringdon**

HYDE PARK—W2 Watson walked from his house in Kensington, through Hyde Park, to Baker Street. **Underground Station: Marble Arch**

PICCADILLY—SW1 In the 1890s, St. James's Hall, Piccadilly, was London's leading concert hall. Holmes and Watson spent one afternoon there, listening to the violinist, Pablo Sarasate, play. **Underground Station: Piccadilly Circus**

THE RESIDENT PATIENT

FLEET STREET—EC4 Holmes and Watson grew weary of their Baker Street sitting room. They took a three-hour stroll through the West End, watching the "ebbs and flows through Fleet Street and the Strand." **Underground Station: Holborn Viaduct**

THE STRAND—WC2 On their three-hour stroll, Holmes and Watson walked down the Strand. **Underground Station: Charing Cross**

MUSEUM OF MANKIND (Former University of London), BURLING-TON GARDENS—W1 Percy Trevelyan received his M.D. degree from the University of London. **Underground Station: Green Park**

CAVENDISH SQUARE—W1 Percy Trevelyan revealed that a medical specialist, who aims high, must start in one of a dozen streets in the Cavendish Square quarter. This is still true today. **Underground Station: Oxford Circus**

HARLEY STREET—W1 Holmes and Watson walked back home from Percy Trevelyan's office on Brook Street. They "had crossed Oxford Street and were halfway down Harley Street" before Watson could get a word out of Holmes. **Underground Station: Regent's Park**

403 BROOK STREET—W1 Blessington set up Dr. Trevelyan in a house at No. 403 Brook Street, and became *The Resident Patient.* Later, Blessington was murdered, and Holmes revealed that he was really Sutton, the bank robber and informant. **Underground Station: Bond Street**

THE ADVENTURE OF THE RETIRED COLOURMAN

THEATRE ROYAL, HAYMARKET—Haymarket Street, SW1 Josiah Amberley had taken two upper circle seats at the Haymarket Theatre. He said he went alone because his wife had a headache. **Underground Station: Piccadilly Circus**

BLACKHEATH TRAIN STATION—SE12 Watson took the train from Blackheath to Lewisham to visit The Haven, Josiah Amberley's house in Lewisham. **BritRail Station: Blackheath**

LEWISHAM—SE13 After Watson went to Lewisham, his observations of Amberley, made Holmes suspicious. **BritRail Station: Hither Green**

LIVERPOOL STATION—EC2 Watson and Josiah Amberley took the 5:20PM train from Liverpool Station to Little Purlington. When Amberley discovered that the ploy was a wild goose chase, they had to wait until the next day to return to London. **Underground Station: Liverpool**

THE ALBERT HALL, KENSINGTON—SW7 Carina was performing at the Albert Hall. Holmes felt that he and Watson should dress, dine, and go to hear her sing. **Underground Station: South Kensington**

A SCANDAL IN BOHEMIA

LANGHAM HOTEL—Portland Place, W1 This very exclusive Victorian hotel has been restored to its former glory. During Holmes's time, the fact that you were a guest at the Langham, automatically, marked you as a gentleman. The King of Bohemia, under the pseudonym Count Von Kramm, stayed at the Langham. **Underground Station: Oxford Circus**

ST. JOHN'S WOOD—NW8 Irene Adler lived in Briony Lodge, St. John's Wood. Holmes devised a scheme to find out where she hid the picture. **Underground Station: St. John's Wood**

INNER TEMPLE—EC4 Godfrey Norton practiced law in the Inner Temple before he married Irene Adler. To escape the King of Bohemia's agents, Holmes included, the couple fled to the Continent. **Underground Station: Temple**

REGENT STREET—W1 Godfrey Norton rushed into Gross and Hankey's in Regent Street. **Underground Station: Piccadilly Circus**

EDGWARE ROAD—W2 The Church of St. Monica was in Edgware Road. Here Godfrey Norton and Irene Adler were married, with a disguised Sherlock as witness. **Underground Station: Edgware Road**

CHARING CROSS RAILWAY STATION—The Strand WC2 Irene Adler and her new husband, Godfrey Norton, left for the Continent from Charing Cross Station. They were trying to escape from the King of Bohemia's agents, Holmes included. Later, whenever Sherlock referred to Irene Adler, he always used the honorable title of "The Woman". **Underground Station: Charing Cross**

THE ADVENTURE OF THE SECOND STAIN

10 DOWNING STREET—SW1 It was from here, one autumn morning, that the Prime Minister came to Baker Street to ask Sherlock's help in recovering a missing document of vital importance. Lord Bellinger was accompanied by Trelawney Hope, Secretary for European Affairs, who had discovered the loss that very morning. **Underground Station: Westminster**

RICHMOND (WHITEHALL) TERRACE—SW1 In my opinion, this was the site of the townhouse occupied by the Right Honorable Trelawney Hope, Secretary for European Affairs, and his wife, Lady Hilda. For the Prime Minister to leave his busy schedule and come to their house for lunch, its location had to be near Downing Street. **Underground Station: Westminster**

GAYFERE (GODOLPHIN) STREET—SW1 Eduardo Lucas lived in the fictitiously named Godolphin Street. In my opinion, its location, "between the river and the Abbey, almost in the shadow of the great tower of the Houses of Parliament," identifies it as Gayfere Street. **Underground Station: Westminster**

HAMMERSMITH—W6 Mitton, Eduardo Lucas's valet, was out the night of the murder. He was visiting a friend in Hammersmith. **Underground Station: Hammersmith**

CHARING CROSS TRAIN STATION—The Strand WC2 The photographs proved, conclusively, that Henri Fournaye and Eduardo Lucas were one and the same. Mme. Fournaye arrived from Paris and attracted much attention at Charing Cross Station. **Underground Station: Charing Cross**

THE ADVENTURE OF SHOSCOMBE OLD PLACE

CURZON STREET—W1 Sir Robert Norberton horsewhipped Sam Brewer, a well-known Curzon Street moneylender, on Newmarket Heath. Brewer was nearly killed. **Underground Station: Green Park**

THE SIGN OF FOUR

CAMBERWELL—SE5 Miss Morstan lived with Mrs. Cecil Forrester in Lower Camberwell. With a twinkle in his eyes, Holmes noted that Watson was eager to visit her there. **Underground Station: Brixton**

LANGHAM HOTEL—Portland Place, W1 This very exclusive Victorian hotel has been restored to its former glory. During Holmes's time, the fact that you were a guest at the Langham automatically marked you as a gentleman. Captain Morstan telegraphed his daughter, Mary, to meet him at the Langham. When she arrived, he was missing. **Underground Station: Oxford Circus**

LYCEUM THEATRE—WC2 Mary Morstan asked Holmes and Watson to accompany her to the Lyceum Theatre. She was following the instructions in a mysteries note she had received. It described her as a "wronged woman."

The Lyceum Theatre is a London landmark. After several fires in the 19th Century, it reopened in 1904. Known for Victorian melodramas and lavish Shakespearean productions, the Lyceum was converted to a dance hall after World War II. It was closed for a number of years before being refurbished and reopened in 1996. **Underground Station: Covent Garden**

THE STRAND—WC2 Holmes, Watson, and Miss Morstan took a cab down the Strand toward the Lyceum. It was a damp September evening, and "The lamps were but misty splotches of diffused light." **Underground Station: Charing Cross**

ROCHESTER ROW—SW1 The coachman, who met them at the Lyceum, drove Holmes, Watson, and Miss Morstan along Rochester Row on their way to Lambeth. **Underground Station: St. James's Park**

VINCENT SQUARE—SW1 On their way down Rochester Row, they passed Vincent Square on the left. **Underground Station: Pimlico**

VAUXHALL BRIDGE ROAD—SW1 They turned left off of Rochester Row onto Vauxhall Bridge Road. **Underground Station: Pimlico**

VAUXHALL BRIDGE—SE11 As they crossed the Thames on Vauxhall Bridge, Holmes remarked that he could catch glimpses of the river. **Underground Station: Vauxhall**

WANDSWORTH (WORDSWORTH) ROAD—SW8 On the Lambeth side of the river, they turned right on Wordsworth Road. **Underground Station: Vauxhall**

LANSDOWNE WAY (PRIORY ROAD)—SW8 From Wandsworth Road, they turned left on Priory Road. In Sherlock's day, the west part of Lansdowne Way was called Priory Road. **BritRail: Wandsworth Road Station**

LANSDOWNE WAY—SW8 They continued on Priory Road as its name changed to Lansdowne Way. **BritRail: Wandsworth Road Station**

PRIORY GROVE (ROAD)—SW8 From Lansdowne Way, they turned right on Priory Road, as it merged with Lark Hall Lane. **Underground Station: Clapham North**

LARKHALL (LARK HALL) LANE—SW4 From Lark Hall Lane they turned east to Stockwell Place. **Underground Station: Brixton**

STOCKWELL PARK WALK (STOCKWELL PLACE)—SW9. As they drove south on Stockwell Place, they were very close to their Cold Harbour Lane destination. **Underground Station: Brixton**

COLDHARBOUR (COLD HARBOUR) LANE—SW9 From the Lyceum Theatre, Holmes, Watson, and Mary had been driven through a labyrinth of Lambeth streets, to Thaddeus Sholto's house in Cold Harbour Lane. There, Sholto told Mary of her father's involvement in *The Sign of Four*.

As you can see, you can follow the four-wheeler's journey from The Lyceum Theatre to Cold Harbour Lane rather precisely, although Conan Doyle changed some of the street names slightly. **Underground Station: Brixton**

KENNINGTON OVAL—SE11 After Sholto's murder, Holmes sent Watson to get Toby from Sherman, the bird stuffer. Holmes said that Toby was "a queer mongrel with the most amazing power of scent." As Holmes and Watson, aided by Toby, attempted to follow the trail of the killers, they found themselves east of the Oval. After reaching a dead end, Toby "waddled around in circles...as if to ask for sympathy in his embarrassment." **Underground Station: Vauxhall**

KENNINGTON LANE—SE11 At one point, in their search east of the Oval, Holmes and Watson found themselves in Kennington Lane. **Underground Station: Oval**

KNIGHT'S WALK (KNIGHT'S PLACE)—SW11 Toby's nose led Holmes and Watson to Knight's Place. Here the trail split in two different directions. At first, they made the wrong choice. **Underground Station: Kennington**

MILES STREET—SE11 Toby, finally, led Holmes and Watson along Miles Street, near the river (the current site of the Flower Market). Toby stopped and began to run forwards and backwards. **Underground Station: Vauxhall**

NINE ELMS—SW8 Holmes, Watson, and the dog followed the wrong trail along Miles Street, from Knight's Place to the timber-yard at Nine Elms. **Underground Station: Vauxhall**

BONDWAY ('BOND STREET')—SE11 Toby led Holmes and Watson near the river, as they passed through Bond Street. Toby stopped and began to run forwards and backwards. He had lost the scent. **Underground Station: Vauxhall**

BLACK PRINCE ROAD (PRINCE'S STREET AND BROAD STREET)—SW8 In Victoria times the lower part of Black Prince Road, which ran down to the Thames, was called Broad Street. Toby led Holmes and Watson through Prince's Street, to Broad Street. There, the quarry had taken a boat. **Underground Station: Vauxhall**

MILLBANK—SW1 At the end of their long walk with Toby, Holmes and Watson took a wherry from Mordecai Smith's boat yard to Millbank, on the north side of the river. **Underground Station: Pimlico**

GREAT PETER STREET—SW1 Holmes wired from the Great Peter Street Post Office (no longer there), to the Baker Street Division of the detective police force. **Underground Station: St. James's Park**

WESTMINSTER STAIRS (BELOW WESTMINSTER BRIDGE)—SW1 In his wire, Holmes told Inspector Jones that he needed a fast police steam launch at the Westminster Stairs at seven o'clock. As it turned out, it was just fast enough. **Underground: Westminster**

WEST INDIA DOCKS—E14 In their police steam launch, Holmes and Watson shot through the Pool of London, past the West India Docks. It took every bit of speed they had to pursue the Aurora. **Underground Station: West India Quay**

ISLE OF DOGS—E14 In their attempt to catch the Aurora, "the fastest boat on the river", Holmes and Watson went past the Isle of Dogs. **Docklands Light Railway Station: Island Gardens**

SILVER BLAZE

PADDINGTON TRAIN STATION—W2 Holmes and Watson left from Paddington Station, on their way to King's Pyland in Dartmoor. They had been asked to solve the mystery of the missing *Silver Blaze*. By timing the telegraph poles, which were placed sixty yards apart, Holmes calculated that the train was traveling at fifty-three and a half miles per hour. **Underground Station: Paddington**

BOND STREET—W1 John Straker, alias William Derbyshire, purchased an expensive costume from Madame Lesurier, a milliner in Bond Street. The bill gave Holmes a clue. **Underground Station: Bond Street**

CLAPHAM JUNCTION—SW11 Colonel Ross, Holmes and Watson passed through Clapham Junction, and Holmes still hadn't finished explaining how he solved the mystery. **Underground Station: Clapham North**

VICTORIA RAIL STATION—SW1 As they arrived at Victoria Station. Holmes invited Colonel Ross to Baker Street for a cigar, and offered to answer all of his questions. **Underground Station: Victoria**

THE ADVENTURE OF THE SIX NAPOLEONS

CHRISTIAN (CHURCH) STREET—E1 Church Street in Stepney is where the firm of Gelder and Co. was located. They were a well-known house in the trade, and had made the busts of Napoleon. After his investigation, Holmes knew that Beppo was the common factor. **Underground Station: Shadwell**

KENNINGTON ROAD—SE11 Dr. Barnicot, an admirer of Napoleon, bought two plaster busts from Morse Hudson, who had a shop in Kennington Road. Both busts were smashed, one in Barnicot's Kennington Road office. **Underground Station: Kennington**

BRIXTON ROAD—SW9 Dr. Barnicot's other bust was smashed in his Lower Brixton Road office. **Underground Station: Brixton**

KENSINGTON HIGH STREET—W8 Harding Brothers had a shop in Kensington High Street. They bought plaster Napoleon busts from Gelder and Co., and sold them to Harker, Brown, and Sandeford. **Underground Station: High Street Kensington**

131 PITT STREET—W8 Mr. Horace Harker, of the Central Press Association, lived at No. 131 Pitt Street, Kensington. His bust was stolen, and a man was murdered on his doorstep. **Underground Station: High Street Kensington**

CAMPDEN HILL (CAMPDEN HOUSE) ROAD—W8 Lestrade said that one of the Napoleon busts had been found in Campden House Road. It was found broken, in the front garden. **Underground Station: Notting Hill Gate**

SAFFRON HILL—EC1 Lestrade told Holmes that they had an inspector, who made a specialty of the Saffron Hill Italian Quarter. He knew Pietro Venucci on sight, and of his connection with the Mafia. **Underground Station: Farringdon**

HAMMERSMITH BRIDGE—W6 Holmes made a pact with Lestrade. "If you come with me to Chiswick tonight…I promise to go to the Italian Quarter with you tomorrow." Late that night, the four-wheeler dropped them near Hammersmith Bridge. **Underground Station: Hammersmith**

CHISWICK—W4 The four-wheeler was at their door at eleven as Holmes and Watson left for 'Laburnum Villa in Chiswick. There, with the help of the owner, Mr. Josiah Brown, they solved the case. **Underground Station: Hammersmith**

THE ADVENTURE OF THE SOLITARY CYCLIST

WATERLOO TRAIN STATION—SE1 Watson caught the 9:13 from Waterloo Train Station. He wanted to be in place, when Violet Smith arrived in Farnham on the 9:50, to see if the bearded cyclist followed her again. **Underground Station: Waterloo**

TOTHILL STREET, SW1 The old Imperial Theatre was part of an amusement complex known as the Royal Aquarium. It covered the site now occupied by the Wesleyan Central Hall, on the north side of Tothill Street. Violet Smith said that her late father "conducted the orchestra at the old Imperial Theatre." **Underground Station: St. James's Park**

THE ADVENTURE OF THE SPECKLED BAND

WATERLOO STATION—SE1 Helen Stoner left Leatherhead on the first train to Waterloo Station. She wanted to consult Holmes on the mysterious death of her twin sister. Later, Holmes and Watson left Waterloo Station on their way to Stoke Moran in Surrey. **Underground Station: Waterloo**

SOMERSET HOUSE—The Strand WC2 In 1883, Somerset House contained the national archives of wills. While investigating the case, Sherlock went there to examine the will of the Stoner sisters' mother. Holmes used the term "Doctors' Common," which was the ancient ecclesiastical court that had kept such records. Although the function had transferred years before, the term remained in common usage. **Underground Station: Temple**

THE STOCK-BROKER'S CLERK

HAMPSTEAD—NW3 Hall Pycroft lived at the fictitious No. 17 Potter's Terrace in Hampstead. **Underground Station: Hampstead**

DRAPERS GARDEN—EC2 Pycroft had a billet at Coxon and Woodhouse's of Drapers Garden. After the problem with the Venezuelan loan, he and the other twenty-six clerks were let go. **Underground Station: Moorgate**

LOMBARD STREET—EC3 After being let go, Pycroft found a position at the great stock-brokerage firm of Mawson & Williams in Lombard Street. **Underground Station: Bank**

PADDINGTON DISTRICT—W2 In this adventure, we find that shortly after his marriage, Watson bought a medical practice in the Paddington district. **Underground Station: Paddington**

A STUDY IN SCARLET

LITTLE GEORGE STREET—SW1 Joseph Stangerson's body was discovered in Halliday's Private Hotel in Little George Street. Above the body was written the word RACHE, in letters of blood. **Underground Station: Westminster**

BRIXTON ROAD—SW9 Holmes and Watson passed Brixton Road on their way to Lauriston Gardens. Gregson, the pick of the Scotland Yarders, called them to examine the site of Enoch J. Drebber's murder. **Underground Station: Brixton**

AMERICAN EXCHANGE—The Strand WC2 A letter in Drebber's pocket was addressed to the American Exchange. In the 1890's, it was located next to the west entry gate of the Charing Cross Rail Station. **Underground Station: Charing Cross**

129 CAMBERWELL—SE5 After his arrival in London from Cleveland, Enoch Drebber bought a hat from John Underwood, a haberdasher at 129 Camberwell Road. **Underground Station: Brixton**

EUSTON STATION—NW1 Drebber and Stangerson had been seen together on the Euston Station platform, presumably waiting for the Liverpool Express. **Underground Station: Euston**

CRITERION BAR—222 Piccadilly, W1 The Criterion has reopened. The restaurant, and its famous long bar, is again the place to meet. It was here that Watson met young Stamford. When Stamford found out that

Watson was looking for someone to go halves on lodging, he reluctantly mentioned Holmes. **Underground Station: Piccadilly Circus**

ST. BARTHOLOMEW'S HOSPITAL—EC1 "St. Bart's", as it is called, is where, in about 1881, young Stamford introduced Watson to Holmes. **Underground Station: St. Paul's**

31 (221B) BAKER STREET—W1 It was in this adventure, where Holmes and Watson first inspected their shared lodgings at Mrs. Hudson's, in Baker Street. It was described as "a couple of comfortable bedrooms and a single large airy sitting-room, cheerfully furnished, and illuminated by two broad windows." In later adventures, we learn that Watson's bedroom was on the floor above, and that Sherlock's bedroom had three doors: one leading to the sitting-room, a second exited to the hallway, and a hidden third door that opened behind the curtains in the sitting-room. **Underground Station: Baker Street**

THE STRAND—WC2 In the 1890s, the Strand was the center of London's West End. Watson recounted that after returning from India, and before meeting Sherlock, he stayed for some time in a private hotel in the Strand. **Underground Station: Charing Cross**

BRIXTON ROAD—SW9 Holmes placed an advertisement in the "Found" column of every morning paper. It read, "In Brixton Road, this morning, a plain gold wedding band, found in the roadway between the White Hart Tavern and Holland Grove. Apply Dr. Watson, 221B, Baker Street, between eight and nine this evening." **Underground Station: Oval**

BRIXTON AND CRANMER ROADS—SW9 The advertisement said that the gold ring was found "in the roadway between the White Hart Tavern and Holland Grove…" Based on this, the White Hart Tavern had to be on the corner of Brixton and Cranmer Roads. **Underground Station: Oval**

PECKHAM—SE15 Mrs. Sawyer answered Holmes's advertisement. She said that her daughter Sally Dennis, who lived in Peckham with her husband Tom, was the one who lost the gold ring. **BritRail: Peckham Rye Station**

HOUNDSDITCH—EC3 Mrs. Sawyer said she lived at an address near Houndsditch. Holmes tried to follow her. When he reached the address, he found that it belonged to a respectable paperhanger named Keswick, who had never heard of Mrs. Sawyer. **Underground Station: Aldgate**

HIGHWAY (RATCLIFF HIGHWAY)—E1 In Holmes's day, this thoroughfare in Stepney had a sinister reputation. The papers were full of the "Brixton Mystery", and the Daily Telegraph mentioned, "the Ratcliff Highway murders." **Underground Station: Stepney**

MUSEUM OF MANKIND (Former University of London)—**Burlington Gardens, W1** In this adventure, we learn that Watson received his M.D. degree from the University of London in 1878. Then, the University was located in Burlington Gardens, the current site of the Museum of Mankind. **Underground Station: Green Park**

THE ADVENTURE OF THE SUSSEX VAMPIRE

OLD JEWRY—EC2 The firm of Morrison, Morrison, and Dodd was located at No. 46 Old Jewry. They remembered Holmes's successful action in the case of "The Matilda Briggs", and referred Mr. Ferguson. **Underground Station: Bank**

MINCING LANE—EC3 Robert Ferguson, of Ferguson and Muirhead, tea brokers of Mincing Lane, was referred to Holmes on a matter of vampires. Holmes looked under V in his great index volume. **Underground Station: Aldgate**

HAMMERSMITH—W6 Holmes found: Victor Lynch, the forger, Vittoria, the circus belle, and Vigor, the Hammersmith wonder. **Underground Station: Hammersmith**

RICHMOND—SW14 Ferguson, in his younger days, played rugby for Richmond. He recognized Watson as fellow rugby player. **Underground Station: Richmond**

BLACKHEATH—SE12 Watson had played on the Blackheath Rugby team. **Underground Station: Greenwich**

OLD DEER PARK—SW14 Ferguson remembered the day he threw Watson into the crowd at the Old Deer Park. **Underground Station: Richmond**

VICTORIA STATION—SW1 Ferguson was relieved when Holmes and Watson agreed to take the 2PM train from Victoria to Lamberley in Sussex. **Underground Station: Victoria**

THE "GLORIA SCOTT"

ADMIRALTY, THE—Whitehall, SW1 The Old Admiralty Offices in Whitehall, are where it was set down that the "Gloria Scott" was lost at sea. No word ever leaked out as to her true fate. **Underground Station: Charing Cross**

THE ADVENTURE OF THREE GABLES

HARROW WEALD—HA1 Mary Maberley asked Holmes to visit her at the Three Gables, her house in Harrow Weald. She had received a very strange offer to buy the house and its contents. Later, the Barney Stockdale Gang burgled the house. **Underground Station: Harrow and Wealdstone**

HOLBORN BAR—EC1 Stone obelisks mark the City boundary at Holborn. Steve Dixie, the Negro bruiser, burst into Baker Street to threaten Holmes. When Holmes mentioned the killing of young Perkins outside the Holborn Bar, the Negro's face turned leaden. Some think that the phrasing indicates the murder took place outside a public establishment in the area, but I think it simply means outside the City, at Holborn Bar. **Underground Station: Chancery Lane**

BOODLE'S—28 St. James's Street, SW1 This gentlemen's club, founded in 1762, has a famous bow window facing St. James's Street. Holmes went to see Langdale Pike, who spent his waking hours in the window, gathering London gossip. **Underground Station: Green Park**

GROSVENOR SQUARE—W1 Holmes and Watson went to see Isadora Klein, the celebrated Spanish beauty and widow of the sugar king. She lived in one of the finest corner-houses on Grosvenor Square. Is it where the London Marriott is now located? **Underground Station: Bond Street**

THE ADVENTURE OF THE THREE GARRIDEBS

CHRISTIE'S AUCTIION HOUSE—8 King Street, SW1 This famous auction house was founded in 1766. Nathan Garrideb lived in an abode of Bohemian bachelors. He rarely left his quarters, except to go to Christie's to bid on additions to his natural history collection. **Underground Station: Green Park**

WATERLOO BRIDGE ROAD—SE1 Holmes discovered that John Garrideb was, in fact, Killer Evens, an American with a sinister and murderous reputation. He came to London in 1893, and shot a man over cards in a nightclub in Waterloo Road in January 1895. **Underground Station: Waterloo**

EDGWARE ROAD—W2 The office of Holloway and Steele, house agents for Nathan Garrideb, was located in Edgware Road. **Underground Station: Edgware Road**

THE VALLEY OF FEAR

CAMBERWELL—SE5 Holmes corresponded with Fred Porlock through the Camberwell post office. Porlock was an associate of Professor Moriarty. Today, the Camberwell post office is in Orpheus Street. **Underground Station: Brixton**

HAMPSTEAD—NW3 Cecil James Barker lived in Hales Lodge, Hampstead. He lied to the police to help his friend, John Douglas, who was later killed by Moriarty. **Underground Station: Hampstead**

VICTORIA STATION—SW1 Inspector McDonald, Holmes, and Watson left from Victoria Station on their way to solve the murder of John Douglas of Birlstone Manor House. **Underground Station: Victoria**

THE ADVENTURE OF THE VEILED LODGER

SOUTH BRIXTON—SW2 Watson went to Baker Street after receiving a hurried note from Holmes. There, he met Mrs. Merrilow of South Brixton. In the late 19th-century, South Brixton was a popular middle-class suburb. **Underground Station: Brixton**

THE ADVENTURE OF WISTERIA LODGE

CHARING CROSS—WC2 On a bleak, windy day, in March 1892, Holmes received a telegram from the Charing Cross telegraph office. It was from Scott Eccles, and read: "HAVE JUST HAD MOST INCREDIBLE AND GROTESQUE EXPERIENCE. MAY I CONSULT YOU?" **Underground Station: Charing Cross**

HIGH HOLBORN—WC1 It was a cold winter evening when Holmes, Watson, and Inspector Baynes set off for Wisteria Lodge. The place was empty, but there was a great deal of clothing, with the stamp of Marx and Co., High Holborn. **Underground Station: Holborn**

BRITISH MUSEUM—Great Russell Street, WC1 Holmes visited the British Museum reading up on Eckermann's "Voodooism and the Negroid Religions." **Underground Station: Tottenham Court Road**

THE YELLOW FACE

CRYSTAL PALACE—SW19 Grant Munro, the hop merchant, disturbed by the actions of his wife, didn't go into the City, but walked as far as the Crystal Palace before returning home. **BritRail: Gipsy Hill Station**

HYDE PARK—W2 Holmes and Watson took an early spring walk in the Park and found that they had missed a client. Their walk could have been in Regent's Park, but I think it was probably Hyde Park. **Underground Station: Marble Arch**

0-595-28114-1

Printed in the United States
41779LVS00004B/32

9 780595 281145